THE ALCHEMY OF
HEALING

THE ALCHEMY OF

HEALING

THE HEALER WAS ALWAYS YOU

FARNAZ AFSHAR

BALBOA.
PRESS
A DIVISION OF HAY HOUSE

Balboa Press books may be ordered through booksellers or by contacting:

Balboa Press
A Division of Hay House
1663 Liberty Drive
Bloomington, IN 47403
www.balboapress.com.au
1-(877) 407-4847

ISBN: 978-1-4525-1076-7 (sc)
ISBN: 978-1-4525-1077-4 (e)

The author would like to hear from you, you can contact her at
the book's website at www.alchemyofhealing.com

Printed in the United States of America

Balboa Press rev. date: 10/04/2013

Acknowledgements and Dedication

I want to start my dedication by giving thanks to Louise Hay for her kind, loving words in *You Can Heal Your Life*, which I discovered by accident (although now I know there are no accidents) at nineteen, in the depths of depression. My eyes were first opened to the power of my thoughts and my journey of self-discovery began.

I want to dedicate this book to Abraham (Esther and Jerry Hicks) for their loving and patient teachings of the Universal Laws that I discovered years later. While I have read widely and studied the works of many teachers on this journey, Abraham's teachings have been by far the most monumental in my recovery from illness to wellbeing.

I am forever grateful and in return hope this book can be a bridge for those not familiar with Abraham's teachings. While my focus is on the subject of health in this book, Abraham's teachings have been fundamental in every other aspect of my life and the lives of those closest to me.

I must clarify that I am not associated with Abraham, not in this physical dimension at least. I am explaining their teachings from my own experiences and interpretation through the years.

Contents

Preface

I wrote this book because it is the book I wanted to read, while in the depths of sadness and hopelessness over my obscure, so called 'incurable' and sometimes un-diagnosable illnesses that slowly began in my teens and grew in my twenties. I wrote this book because it's the book I needed to read when I couldn't walk, sleep or sit from chest stiffness, mind-blowing back pain and sharp hip pains. I wrote this book because it's the book I needed when at 3am I'd constantly wake up from agonising pain, but incapable of even getting myself out of bed. I wrote this book for every time I received a new diagnosis of something else wrong with my liver, lungs or stomach. I wrote this book because it's the book I wish someone would have handed me, every time I couldn't look in the mirror because of severe cystic acne, for every time someone reminded me I was breaking out (as if I didn't know?), for every time my specialist handed me a bottle of pills (to magically 'balance' my hormones), for every time my dad concluded my skin condition was surely because I was eating too much chocolate (even though I rarely consumed any, and my sister who consumed ten times that amount has never had a single pimple). I wrote this book because it's the book I wish I had found when I was too self-conscious to go on dates because of my skins condition. I wrote this book because it contains what I didn't know when I was spending thousands of dollars on ultrasounds, blood tests, x-rays, doctors, chiropractic and physio sessions, endocrinologists, sports physicians, homeopaths, naturopaths, iridologists, acupuncturist consultations, the latest pills, anti-blemish washes, soaps, retinol lotions and toners. I wrote this book because I am certain I am not the only person on this planet who wants reassurance that healing is on its way. Because it may help people, young and old realise they hold the key to their body's wellbeing. To help you take your power back.

I feel great appreciation for the time you are taking to read this book, and I hope it can answer some of your questions. My intention is to reach out to those who are in the same place I was at. Those wanting wellness, who are not able to find health through conventional pill-popping medicine. If only one person is able to find relief from illness with the assistance of this book, I have accomplished my mission. You are loved more than you will ever know, and I hope you become one step closer to realising your worth, as I have through this journey.

Introduction

What if I told you, you have created your current physical ailments? You may call me a few names I can't repeat here, but that won't stop me from pointing out the truth as I have come to discover it. It may surprise you, but you have created your current illness, or any other health crisis you are in. The obvious fact is no one would choose to be sick. No one would choose disease over wellbeing. The reality is, however, you have created the current bodily state (unknowingly) by becoming a match to whatever you are currently experiencing.

But I'm not here to blame you or make you feel any worse. My intention for writing this book is to give you back the power social conditioning has taken away from you. By making us feel like victims of circumstances, be it incorrect diet, not enough exercise, genetic background or other environmental factors, the world around us has brainwashed us into believing our wellbeing is only in the hands of expensive medication and health care professionals who know more than we do. After all, they have studied in universities for many years, and are better equipped to advise us than anyone, right? This illusion that permeates our world has made people rely on external help and institutions for wellbeing. Not only have we not been taught our enormous power as creators in our own lives, but we have been made to feel incapable of curing ourselves. In today's society we are bombarded with the latest pill, potion or cream that promises to target headaches, back pain, diabetes, heart disease, osteoporosis, hip pain, acne, arthritis, allergies, ulcers, colds, flu . . . and a thousand more health problems. The list is endless.

Walk into a pharmacy or your local supermarket and you'll find countless products that claim to fight just acne alone. And new ones are developed each day, with more promises. Yet there are millions of people (adults as well as youths) not having any success with any of these products. And that's just one skin disease.

Fear not. If all the thousands of products applied, consumed, inhaled or injected do not solve your health issues; there is a vast variety of surgical procedures that will cut the problems from your body. We now live in a world where there are more specialists and scientists, more health care accessible to more people, yet there is more disease than ever before. Every day you turn on the news and some new virus is discovered or a rare form of cancer is being 'fought'. Ask yourself why. With all the advancement in technology and the raised standard of living, why is the variety of illnesses growing exponentially in the world today?

Simply put, we do not know the true power of our conscious mind, and its ability to manifest ease or dis-ease in our lives and bodies. We have been conditioned to think that swallowing a little white pill (mass-produced by large pharmaceutical companies) will magically 'target' the diseased area. Of course there is big business in every form of illness or disease. So as well as you feeling bad physically and emotionally, there is money in your ill-health for those companies. There is a lot of money being made out of your current bodily conditions. That's why you are often made to feel like you are missing out on a 'potential cure' if you don't have the latest product being marketed through TV, the radio, Internet or any billboard you drive by.

A prevention of 'ease' in the body is disease. When I first came across this concept, it didn't really hit home until I experienced it in my own body. And I didn't really understand how I was preventing 'ease' in my own body until a few years later when the conventional medical dog-and-pony show was no longer helping me. I don't mean to play down the great work of some health practitioners and surgeons in saving lives. Modern medicine is perfect for emergencies and giving your body immediate stability so that you can freely turn your focus to changing your emotional state. As long as you heal emotionally, medicine is fine. It's only because society today places so much emphasis on the physical action of medicine and ignored the important metaphysical aspect of healing, that true healing is not experienced by many.

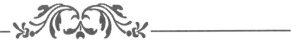

"Reality is merely an illusion, albeit a
very persistent one."

—Albert Einstein

You don't know what you don't know

If you tie the legs of a newborn to a wheelchair long enough, the child will not learn to walk like other children. And when untied from the shackles of the chair, as she has spent all her life confined to the chair and never became conscious of her ability to walk, she will not be able to walk the first time she tries. Not because she doesn't have legs or the ability to use them, but because she has not practised using them long enough for it to become a deep belief. If she now does not practise strengthening her legs and walking, she will spend the rest of her life believing and hence living a lie.

While the example above is exaggerated to make a point, it is not so far from the truth when it comes to the beliefs we let get planted into our minds by those around us as soon as we're born.

As you will discover from my journey and research into true wellbeing, there are a lot of beliefs we must first question before we are freed from the mental shackles we live with on a daily basis. What is a belief anyway? Beliefs are essentially agreements (personal and collective) about reality that create your life experiences. I will share with you why health, vitality, beauty, flexibility, strength, insert-your-desire-here, is 99% about your emotions. The rest of the 1% just comes naturally once you heal emotionally.

In Part 1, I cover my own health struggles and why modern medicine was not helping me, how I discovered my path and was able to finally heal myself after years of illness and discomfort.

In Part 2, I go into more detail about the path I took that finally lead to my healing, and what I have come to know for sure about conventional and alternative medicine, self-healing and wellness. I have shared everything I personally did to allow my wellbeing and have suggested fun exercises to speed up your healing in the most enjoyable way possible. At the end of the book I have listed a Cheat Sheet with summaries and tips of the learning discussed. These will refresh your memory and can be used as quick reminders throughout your day. You are just an emotion away from the healthy body you have always wanted.

This book is dedicated to answering questions about why we make ourselves sick and why we are the only ones who can heal ourselves, from my personal experience as someone who has spent a decade trying every solution under the sun to heal. And after much searching and agony, I finally came to the conclusion that there is something greater at play. There is something exponentially bigger than me guiding my wellbeing, and no amount of trying through physical action can bring about the health I crave for until I become well emotionally.

In order to respect the privacy of the various doctors and health care professionals I've dealt with during my journey, I have used aliases instead of their real names. My intention is not to defame anyone but to tell my story as objectively as possible.

"Where there is ruin, there is hope for a treasure."

—Rumi (Persian Sufi mystic and poet)

PART 1

How It All Began

In Part 1 I go over all the health problems I personally experienced while searching for healing and provide a background to how I discovered my path. I felt it was useful to explain why I am so certain that healing can only be initiated from within, and how I have come to this clear understanding.

CHAPTER 1

Traumatic Teens

Growing up, I was very lucky to have a loving family, but high school was not easy. I was bullied from age thirteen through to age fifteen for looking different to the other girls in my school. I wasn't blonde or blue-eyed like everyone else, instead I had black hair and olive skin, I wasn't allowed to shave my legs and I ate foreign foods for lunch. I immediately felt different as I began high school, and was a perfect target for bullies from day one. I did have a few friends who did not participate in tormenting me, but most of my class made my life hell on a daily basis for two years. And unfortunately my school (like many other schools) did nothing about the bullying, no matter how concerned my parents were.

I distinctly remember crying in my room on school nights, wishing I didn't have to go to school tomorrow. I remember one night in the midst of sadness thinking I'd rather die than return to that environment. Don't worry, this is not a sympathy request and I am not trying to defame or blame anyone in any way. I am merely setting the scene for explaining where some of my earlier illnesses stemmed from. While two years may not seem long, the daily torments I experienced still haunted me into my twenties.

Within a short period of time, severe acne started developing on my face. My parents initially brushed it off as just being teenage hormones. This was the start of my acne problems. They took me to a doctor who ran tests and concluded I had Polycystic Ovary Syndrome (PCOS) that was causing the acne (and unbalanced hormones). She prescribed the contraceptive pill and said it would balance my hormones in six months and I could then stop taking it. We wanted a second opinion and went to see an endocrinologist, who also had no other suggestion than to prescribe the pill. He did not know the cause of PCOS and so concluded it must be genetic (although no one in my family has ever been diagnosed with this syndrome). Any illness that science does not understand well is labelled 'genetic', it seems.

If you're reading this and thinking that acne does not classify as a disease, it is a form of skin disease, albeit a common one. And because it is so common, we have learnt to accept it as normal, especially in teenagers. While it is not life-threatening, there are hundreds of millions of people suffering from it, from children to middle-aged adults. And a multi-billion-dollar industry runs off these people's unhappiness. The other issue with acne is that it is an indicator of a bigger internal imbalance we don't often know about, it's not just about vanity.

The Law of what?

At that stage of my life, I knew nothing about the Law of Attraction (LOA) and why I was being bullied in school. I did not understand that I was attracting the mean girls that were making me feel bad because at some level I was not feeling good about myself. And I most certainly did not know that the acne and PCOS were a consequence of my negative emotions and thoughts.

If this is the first time you are hearing about the LOA, it may sound strange that I am taking responsibility for what was happening to me at such a young age. And I can confirm it wasn't until I was in my mid-twenties and had been on this journey of self-discovery that I actually realised that everything we experience in our lives is our own doing.

I was first introduced to the idea that we could influence our reality in high school, around seventeen. I was watching the Oprah show and her guest Dr Phil said something that has stuck with me ever since:

> "There is no reality, only perception. What you believe to
> be true about yourself, you will live."

I thought, wow! How can that be? Is it really possible? So I could change my reality by altering my beliefs? I was blown away by what I had heard. I wanted to know more, and that's how my interest in self-development began. At that stage in my life I didn't see personal growth as anything spiritual; it was more of a way of attaining what I wanted—getting from A to B as quickly as I could. I purchased Dr Phil's book *Self Matters* and started working towards finding my 'authentic' self. I began reading many other books by others on self-development like Anthony Robbins, Robert Kyosaki, Napoleon Hill, Charles F. Haanel, Wallace Wattles, Dale Carnegie, Donald Trump, Paul Hanna, John Gray, Suze Orman, Shakti Gawain, Anne Hartley, David J. Schwartz, Al Koran, Vivienne James, Lois P. Frankel, James Allen, and the list goes on. But most self-development books are very much focused on having a strategy, setting goals, working hard, stepping outside your comfort zones, getting financial education, building a network of people, increasing your self-confidence, and only helped me get so far.

I can heal my life?

After reading all those self-development books I still didn't know what the recipe for changing my reality was. Not until I came across a book that changed my life. I remember it as though it was yesterday. I was nineteen, depressed and in my first year of university, studying software engineering. I had recently realised software engineering was not what I imagined it to be, but I had studied so hard in school to be accepted into such a competitive degree and the fear of dropping out and being labelled a 'quitter' was too great. I hated my course with a passion, yet being the persistent girl that I was, I decided I'd continue and finish the five years. The resentment I felt for my degree and my insistence to continue it was tearing me up emotionally. I had also recently been hurt by a guy I cared for, so I felt rejected, unloved, hopeless, unworthy and plain stupid. The tension inside me began to show up in constant colds and flu, to the point where my family doctor David (who in retrospect I can see was very wise) told me it was stress related and that I should take some time off university and relax. I didn't listen and decided to follow the very rational path of finishing my degree on time.

I was feeling particularly bad one day, and decided to go for a run around the block thinking it would make me feel better. I began to slow down in front of the local Salvation Army (in Australia these stores sell second-hand goods to raise money for charity). I suddenly felt the urge to walk into the store. Now at nineteen this was the last store I wanted to be seen in. I had only ever donated clothes to them and Mum had volunteered there, but I had never set foot into the shop myself. But for whatever reason I felt compelled to walk in and, like a person under a spell, I walked directly to the corner where a single bookshelf stood. Most of the shelves were empty. There were only about thirty books in total. Without thinking about it, I placed my index finger on the first book spine that took my attention. It was a brightly-coloured book called *You Can Heal Your Life* by Louise Hay. I pulled it out and read the back cover. I was intrigued by the possibility that if I change my thoughts, my life could be healed. I thought to myself that it was worth a try. I was willing to try anything at that point. I guess that's why they say when you hit rock-bottom, the only way is up. It was priced $2, and while I had no purse with me, there happened to be a

$2 coin in the pocket of my running shorts. It's interesting how things worked out that day.

I bought it, read it and applied it diligently. Louise's book was like a breath of fresh air. At this stage I didn't know what to expect, but I hoped for a change. I did have a good habit of recording everything in a journal. So I recorded all the exercises from Louise's book in my journal. After doing all the exercises (which were mostly affirmation-based), I put the book away and went on with my life.

The turning point

Time went by and I forgot about the book. Then six months later I came across my journal and went through it. I came across the exercises from Louise's book and was shocked by my responses from six months previously. I was literally gobsmacked by what I was reading. I couldn't believe that I myself had written those answers. In just six months my expectations of life had raised considerably. I realised that not only had I changed a lot from where I was six months ago, but my life had also changed as a consequence of Louise's teachings. And the proof was in my hands. At that point I learned the importance of documenting your personal progress, because we humans seem to be very forgetful. And while forgetting bad incidents is good, we sometimes forget the good we asked for in the past, which has come about into our lives since.

This day was a turning point in my life. I had solid evidence that it is possible to change your life and your experiences through positive affirmations. I had gone from having very negative perceptions of relationships (taught to me by my well-meaning mother), to expecting relationships to work out for me. I had gone from seeing no future for myself, to seeing some happiness coming my way. So I began practising the affirmations more from then onwards. And slowly more and more things began to change in my life. But being in my early twenties, all I really wanted to do was finish my degree and start my career. I wanted to be like other girls my age having fun. I didn't want to be writing affirmations every day. It had become a chore. As life started to go well for me (socially and financially) and I became more confident as a young adult, I eventually grew out of this practise. In retrospect I can see I had turned writing affirmations into a task, something I had to do, on top of everything else, which is why it lost its appeal for me. Plus there was no emotion behind the affirmations once they became a daily task on my To Do list, so their effectiveness started to decline.

In part 2, I will explain in detail why thoughts have no power if they are not backed by strong emotion, and the same applies to daily affirmations. At this stage of my life I was still under the impression that modern medicine would heal all illnesses, and I didn't have any concept of emotions leading to disease. I was young and inexperienced, yet life was about to give me a crash-course on illness and recovery.

Pill-popping

By this stage I had switched to seeing a second specialist, Ben, who was a professor of endocrinology and with years of research in PCOS. I was hoping he was better than my first specialist and with his wisdom could resolve my hormonal situation and excessive breakouts. He conducted some initial blood tests and continued to prescribe the same pill. I was still breaking out and had also developed hirutism. Because the pill was no longer controlling the breakouts, Ben put me on Spironolactone to help fight the breakouts and reduce excessive hair. So every day I was taking two white pills, the pill from age fifteen and Spironolactone from age nineteen.

Concurrently I was not happy about being on drugs forever. I tried alternative therapies such as remedial shiatsu, energy therapy, Chinese medicine and cupping, and while they felt good at the time of treatment, I didn't see any long-term results. I also tried a few times to go cold turkey, only for my skin to become horrid within a few weeks. So I'd give up and go back on medication.

The wake-up call

In early 2008 I watched a television documentary on the psychological side effects of the pill on women, and how their pheromones were badly manipulated by it. They found women on the pill were more likely to select mates whose genes are not compatible with theirs, and in extreme cases this resulted in deformities in their conceived babies. Apparently this is because of the constant pregnant state induced by the pill. Unknowingly you are drawn to men who may not be genetically compatible because your body thinks it's already pregnant and doesn't need a genetically compatible mate as a priority. In other cases women who had met their mates on the pill, married and then stopped the pill to conceive, would only find they were no longer attracted to their partners. This was a scary wake-up call for me, after being on the pill for almost a decade and having had a history of attracting the wrong type of guys. It was that program coming into my experience accidentally (although there are no accidents) that made me seriously decide to stop the pill. At that stage I did not know my severe anger was also a symptom of the pill. I continued to research the production of synthetic estrogen, the huge $22-billion-a-year industry built around it, and the horrific side effects of this drug on women.

Taking 'action' to heal

So I set out to get off the medication, thinking with the guidance of a doctor it would be easy. I cancelled my bi-annual specialist appointments, and went to see a family doctor. My doctor however did not know enough about the recent research to comment or reassure me. I did my own research and found out it could take up to a year for all traces of the pill to leave your body. I slowly began to rid my body of the medication. First I stopped Spironolactone. It took about six months for it to leave my body, and sure enough my skin started breaking out severely again. Then the pill was stopped and my facial acne became horrific. My skin was so bad (and those who know me know I'm fairly confident) I was embarrassed to leave the house some days. I initially fell for all the glossy ads and purchased all the well-known anti-acne skincare products I could. I also heard IPL kills bacteria in the acne, is skin clearing and also removes excessive hair, so I spent several thousand dollars on that. I even tried prescription creams like Differin hoping that would work, but no luck.

But I was determined to find a solution, so I started reading as much as I could on female hormones. My doctor back in high school who started me on the pill in the first place had convinced me and my parents I had hormonal issues that would be 'easily balanced' by the pill within six months. Ten years later I was still taking twice the medication and not seeing any lasting improvements. At this stage I knew that it's very possible a slight temporary hormonal imbalance back when I was fifteen could have become a self-fulfilling prophecy ten years later. After all Ben, who I was seeing a few times a year and paying huge consultation fees to, had not conducted a blood test to check my hormones for years. All he did was top up my pill bottles each time he saw me.

By that time my desire to find a real solution to my hormonal imbalances and skin breakouts was stronger than ever. I was determined not to give up. Over the next two years I read hundreds of blogs, books, publications, anything I could find on female hormones by people who claimed to have the answers and other women documenting their journeys. What I discovered was terrifying. I found out the hormones fed to women in contraceptive pills are synthetic and some sources said these hormones are sometimes derived from pregnant horses' urine.

This made me wonder why synthetic hormones were being used when naturally-occurring hormones are plentiful in nature. I later discovered that pharmaceutical companies cannot sell naturally-occurring estrogen in their pills. There is no profit in this, as no one can patent a natural substance. So in order to patent their estrogens (and hence profit), the molecular structure of naturally-occurring estrogens is modified. The problem with this practice is that our hormone receptors are designed to respond to natural estrogens. Instead the modified synthetic estrogens, Xenoestrogens, block our hormone receptors and cause havoc in the body by preventing the body from absorbing any natural estrogens available, so much so that it can take at least six months for the remaining Xenoestrogens to leave a female body after stopping the pill. My doctors and specialists had not just stopped my body from producing its own estrogens naturally, but they had blocked my hormone receptors from receiving any natural estrogen that was available in my body.

So from the age of fifteen to twenty-five my trust had been in health professionals who had kept my body in a constant state of induced pregnancy. I then found out women on the pill for long periods of time have been found to have problems conceiving. It just got worse and worse. I went through an extremely angry phase soon after finding out the truth about the medication pharmaceutical companies give doctors to recommend. I was furious that for patent reasons they modify the molecular structure of naturally-occurring estrogen so that it can be sold to women. I was angry with the medical professionals prescribing these dangerous pills to young girls. I was furious that I had been encouraged to turn to pills and harsh toxic acne products that help fuel a multi-billion dollar industry. The greater issue is that the pills and products are not really healing the cause of the disease, but trying to shut down the symptoms.

Naturally, as these thoughts dawned on me, I became more and more angry. I was angry at myself for trusting those people. I felt betrayed and ripped off. I was angry at my parents for not looking at alternative medicine for me, I was angry at the pharmaceutical companies for making huge profits from me and other women. I experienced a variety of emotions, which I now know is normal from Abraham's teachings. These included denial initially, fear, anger, remorse, and then eventually acceptance. And once again I wished I was like other girls my age, and not spending every waking minute researching the subject of health. Why couldn't my body just be balanced like other people my age? Why did this have to happen to me?

More manifestations of dis–ease

Concurrently to the medication I was on for my hormones and skin, I also had occasional pains in my chest that began in high school. On damp, rainy days I would get a sharp pain in my chest where I could exhale but not inhale. It was like my lungs were being squeezed from the inside. I saw a number of different doctors about this as well. One night in January 2007, I went to bed feeling normal and woke up early the next morning with tremendous disabling pain in my upper body. It was winter and I was in New Jersey at the time, and my family assumed I had just caught a chill. I returned to a hot Sydney summer and experienced a few episodes of the sharp pains again. I thought it was my mattress, so I started sleeping on the ground. That didn't help either.

I visited a physiotherapist and he recommended I invest in an all latex bed. I did that and the pain got better for a little while, then returned stronger. I then consulted with a chiropractor, who found out I had a slight scoliosis (5%). She said if I had gone to see her ten years later, the scoliosis would be so bad I'd need an operation to be able to keep walking. She was able to help my back's misalignment (from heavy school bags), but had no explanation or solution for the sharp pains in my body. All she could recommend was I only sleep on my back with a pillow under my knees. She gave me some lower back exercises to do, but that did not resolve the disabling pains.

In 2009 another unhealthy relationship left me feeling damaged. Within a month a sharp pain appeared in my hip. It was so intense I couldn't walk. I'd literally limp to work and back, at twenty-six.

At this stage I could not see the correlation between my emotional state and my physical state. I still did not have enough awareness that my negative emotions were creating havoc in my body. Not only was I unable to participate in any physical activity like exercise, I couldn't even sit up some days. Gradually my body was beginning to stiffen. But I still had hope that doctors held the key to my health problems. I was referred to a sports physician who was able to pinpoint the hip muscles that caused the pain, but had no solution for it other than prescribing Voltaren for pain relief. He conducted blood tests and found I had rheumatoid arthritis. He admitted that in some patients this condition disappears on its own, while in some it worsens. I had already begun working towards ridding my body of the pill and Spironolactone, so the last thing I wanted to do was pop Voltaren for the rest of my life.

In the process of getting off the pill, I asked for a full check-up and my doctor found I was severely Vitamin D deficient, with high cholesterol and had elevated Gamma GT levels (similar to that of an alcoholic or drug addict). But she had no explanation for the elevated GT levels. She asked if I drank alcohol or consumed drugs, which I did not. She predicted my liver had been damaged due to the length of time I was on the pill (a decade). Once again there was no solution for this problem, other than wait and see. And if the GT levels continued to rise, the only other 'solution' was to take more medication, and who knows what the side effects of that would be on my other organs. My list of ailments was growing rapidly. As if PCOS, scoliosis, back pain, excessive acne, hirutism and rheumatism wasn't enough, I also had liver problems.

I researched other cultures and what they use. It seems many cultures use fenugreek, fennel and saw palmetto to balance hormones and, hence, skin. I started consuming these herbs, based on the recommendations I found, for about six months but there was still no change in my body.

I continued looking at alternative ways of healing. A colleague recommended I see a naturopath who had helped her conceive successfully. I really was open to anything and desperate for a solution. The naturopath said I needed to detox my body. She was convinced my excessive breakouts where due to my diet. She also ran more tests and found out I was extremely iodine deficient (normal levels are above 100 and mine was thirteen). She looked at my blood and concluded I must have a leaky gut syndrome, as none of the supplements I was consuming were being absorbed by my body. The detox she placed me on for four weeks was severe and aimed at removing toxins from my body and clearing my skin.

I did a diet haul, removed all dairy, sugar, salt, white carbohydrates, processed or packaged foods, red meats, increased my vitamin intake, checked my thyroid and iodine levels, and detoxed my liver and kidneys. I ate only organic chicken and eggs, mostly vegetables and fruit. Fish oil, Zinc, Vitamin D, Probiotics, Iodine, alfalfa chlorine extracts were just a small selection of the supplements I was taking to alkalise my body and reduce its acidity. Months later I was still breaking out as before, and about $700 down in my bank account. Once again nothing else had changed. The only benefit of this expensive exercise was my new-found appreciation for vegetables, and I increased my consumption.

The more action I took to heal my body, the more illnesses I was diagnosed with. The more illnesses I knew about, the more depressed I'd feel. The more negative I felt, the more illnesses developed . . . it was a vicious cycle.

As I didn't see any results from the naturopath, I attempted to alkalise my body on my own. Some research I did pointed to excessive acidity in the body causing the acne and arthritic pains, so I thought I had found the solution once and for all. I purchased a water filtration system that promised to alkalise drinking water and, hence, my body. I spent another $500 on that but my skin did not clear and my back did not improve. The research behind the water claimed that most bodily disease is due to excess acid, which the water filter was meant to reduce. Another few months went by and not only did nothing improve, I started losing hope.

My back pain was becoming more and more severe, to the point where there were days I'd wake up from the pain at 3am but not be able to lift myself out of bed. At that stage I had become so accustomed to horrid skin, if there was a day when new acne didn't appear I'd get excited. I had reached a point where I was willing to try anything, except give in to more medication and continue to live a lie now that I knew the truth. I heard about homeopathy, and thought maybe that would work. A friend's husband had had great success with his Multiple Sclerosis (MS) using homeopathy so I thought it was worth a try. I read a lot about it and how it's aimed at healing you vibrationally, which made sense to me. I intrinsically knew there must be something deeper causing my problems, but I didn't know what exactly. I thought I was a fairly positive person and couldn't see what was really causing my illnesses.

I consulted with a homeopath and tried every remedy he recommended for well over a year. He discovered a number of other imbalances in my gut which he was able to resolve, but he could not heal the original health issues I had consulted him about. My success with the homeopath was very similar to my previous attempts towards physical healing. He was able to find more things wrong with me than

I knew about, and his remedies had no lasting success with my acne, hormones or back pain.

Giving up

As I had not had any major success with anything I had tried for many years, I eventually became sick of trying and just gave up. I had also spent a small fortune on all the various medications and health care professionals, so I really couldn't afford it any longer. And I'm not someone who gives up that easily, which is probably evident from the many avenues I explored to find healing. In retrospect, it's quite clear that the more I tried to find the solution to my problems, the more problems found me. As the saying goes, "energy flows where attention goes". As soon as you notice a problem, the LOA will bring you more problems to notice. Unfortunately our society is not versed enough with this knowledge, and instead we are encouraged to focus on our problems in order to solve them. But the truth is, even if you take the one subject that isn't working and focus on it, it will multiply rapidly to the point where most subjects in your life become problematic.

Now, if you are like me and want to feel in control of your life, being told to 'ignore' an issue, especially if it's as big as a health problem just doesn't work or seem rational. How can I pretend I'm not in pain when every step causes a shooting pain through my body? In the next chapter, I will explain how I overcame this problem by raising my emotional state. It's a lot simpler than you think.

"The wound is the place where the Light enters you."

—Rumi

CHAPTER 2

How I Discovered My Path

A t this stage it was the end of 2010 and I was in the process of packing to move into a new property I was buying. I still had the excessive acne (at twenty-seven), my back and upper chest were still sore and stiff every day when I woke up and randomly during the day, and the hip pain was still around, some weeks more than others. While going through some old boxes I came across the notes I had made during the 2009 lecture by Abraham Hicks in Sydney. I had written: 'When you go against the natural stream of your life, you get sick. All forms of dis-ease are due to you not allowing the stream to flow.' I thought maybe this was the answer I've been searching for. By that stage in my life I did feel like I had been struggling upstream for a long time. Why did I not realise this years ago when I first read Abraham's books? Why did it take so long? How did I lose my way? For me this was a new idea, even though I had written it down myself years back. Perhaps I was too young at the time to fully grasp the idea. But more importantly how do I stop going against my stream now and start going down the stream?

I needed to learn as much as I could about this stream so I started listening to Abraham Hicks's lectures on the way to work and back. (I had purchased their CDs years back, but never really diligently listened to them.) And more importantly, I started applying their advice. I wasn't expecting much progress health-wise, seeing as nothing else had worked so far. But their teachings made me feel good, I couldn't help but follow the good feeling. And slowly I started caring about the way I felt. I began listening to my heart for the first time in years and it felt so right.

In part 2, I go into the details of Abraham's teachings as I applied them to my life and how you can do the same.

The first result I saw in my life when I started going down the stream was actually not in my body but in the settlement of my property. For most of the purchase period I was on the phone every two days either with my lawyers, the real estate agents or with my mortgage broker trying to resolve the many problems the settlement was having. Within a few weeks of caring about my emotions and becoming happier, I noticed that on days when I was feeling really good about myself and life in general, settlement procedures with various parties went smoothly. Then on days when I was feeling rotten, I'd get calls from each party with bad news, the contracts were lost in the post, the selling party became problematic, the list was endless. Then my mood would change (something good in my life would take my focus away from the issues) and the property problems would resolve themselves quickly. This happened about five or six times in the course of a few weeks before I noticed a pattern emerge. My initial reaction was, could it be a coincidence that when I feel good the property purchase runs smoothly, and when I feel bad it doesn't? But the reality I was living could not just be a coincidence. A coincidence doesn't keep happening over and over again. In fact I no longer believe in coincidences any more. I think the only reason we call something a coincidence is because we don't yet fully understand the connection between the way we feel and the resulting manifestations.

Within two weeks of feeling happier, the back pain I used to get up with every morning was gone. I remember one morning suddenly realising I had not had any pain for the past few days. It was strange, initially I thought it was my imagination. It felt so nice to get up and not feel crippled. But more importantly it felt good to feel good. At this stage I still didn't know my better-feeling body was because I was taking care of my emotions, I just knew it felt good to be able to move without stiffness and pain. But as I kept watching how I felt, and trying to feel better, I noticed things go my way more and more.

After about a month, my skin started showing noticeable improvement. It wasn't totally clear, but instead of multiple painful pimples per day, I'd get them per week. There was no change in my diet or lifestyle, other than I was happier. After years of looking for a solution and following every bit of advice without luck, this felt like a miracle. I was getting hooked on Abraham's teachings, and my family started to notice.

I was very happy. So I continued to hold a positive outlook on my life and look for more things to feel good about as Abraham advised. I noticed I felt best when I listened to my heart on any subject. Now, for me, this could be doing something as simple as having a nap on the weekend, and I'd wake up feeling reenergised. Sometimes it was staying home on Saturday nights to read my favourite book, instead of going out. Or going to my favourite beach on Sunday and doing nothing at all. The happier I got, the more my health improved, and my skin started clearing rapidly. And the back stiffness and hip pains I'd had for years were a thing of the past. How do you feel when you listen to your heart? Have you, like so many, shut that calling out so much that it's almost hard to hear? Have a think about how it feels to listen to your gut.

"Let yourself be drawn by the stronger pull of that which you truly love."

—Rumi

Go where you are pulled

In the process of listening to my heart, I stopped forcing myself to socialise with friends that did not have my best interests at heart. Until twenty-six, I felt peer pressure to dress up and go to the most popular clubs with my girlfriends, even though I never really had fun. It was an endless waste of energy, money and precious time. While I would never judge someone else who chooses these things, at that stage of my life it was not serving me. I felt I needed something deeper, something more grounding. So I stopped trying so hard to make these relationships work. I allowed life to take care of them for me. If a friendship is going to end because one of us no longer wants to go clubbing, then it's best it ends sooner rather than later. I started practising yoga early in the morning, and it felt so good. I stopped spending hours and hours shopping and looking for the latest sale. One particular friend could not deal with the changes I was making in my life, and I remember her saying "You've done a complete 180 degrees from who you were before" in criticism.

In the process of allowing, instead of trying, I lost a number of friends who were not in harmony with the newer, happier me. But that was okay. I knew that the people who would remain in my life through this personal transition were the ones I ultimately wanted around. I think I always knew deep inside who these people were, but I hadn't listened to that inner voice. Instead I followed the status quo and remained in those shallow friendships until it got to the point where I couldn't deny it any more. The discord in my body was quite strong, although at the time I didn't realise my emotional turmoil was leading to the aches and pains, the excessive breakouts and unbalanced hormones. I believe there is immense benefit to knowing who in your life is authentic. And as you become more of who you really are, as you listen to your calling more and more, your life will open up to more authentic people. After all, you draw into your life people who are vibrationally in synch with you. As I did one thing that felt good, I'd come across something else that would feel good. In the next few years I started taking art classes which I'd wanted to take since high school. Ever since high school I had stopped myself from following my heart. So finally at twenty-seven I started to understand what it felt like to go where I was being pulled, towards what felt good and really care about my feelings. I began to taste how good it feels to be happy, truly happy. Living a shallow unconscious life was no longer ringing my bell.

So I became even keener to apply Abraham's teachings. Naturally there was much more than good health I wanted to manifest. We all have many desires in every area of our lives that we want to see fulfilled, and as soon as my body started to recover, I remembered all my other goals.

A few months later the happiness came to a screeching halt when seemingly out of nowhere my face would breakout again, or the sharp pains would return. And my hormones were certainly not any more balanced. Of course at the time I thought the recurrence was out of nowhere. But after much trial and error, and paying close attention to how I felt in any moment during the day, I became more sensitive to my emotions and started noticing that any time I had any strong negative thoughts about someone or myself, the next day I'd be limping from hip pain. It was bizarre and took me many months to figure out what was happening. My acne was similar. When I had a mild negative thought about myself or other people, I'd get a visit of pimples the next day. Any time at work my colleagues started gossiping about another colleague, if I joined in I would breakout the next day.

I didn't want to believe it at first. I was in denial. To be honest it seemed a bit absurd, because I'd never heard of other people breaking out after a gossip-fest. The truth is I am not with anyone else all day long to know how their discord expresses itself. I certainly know these people were not the happiest bunch of folks, but I guess neither was I at the time. That's why I was rendezvousing with them in the first place. They were at my vibrational level.

I initially felt angry at this anomaly I was experiencing. But after it kept recurring over and over again, I couldn't deny it any longer. When something as bad as cystic acne is on your face, there is no way to deny its presence. And after I noticed the pattern of negative thoughts/judgement/criticism about others or myself leading to breakouts, the breakouts showing up was a reminder to focus on what I wanted and not give attention to the negativity I'd come across during the day. I must admit I felt pretty discouraged initially because after seeing my good progress, I was faced with an obstacle I didn't know how to get around. I thought: how am I ever going to heal if even being in the presence of critical people causes me to breakout? I then began to worry about breaking out each time someone around me had started a negative conversation about someone else, to the point where I would physically get up and leave the room if I could.

One thing I did have control over was my own thoughts, I could decide to focus on seeing the good in people, regardless of what went on around me, and not personally engage in gossip of any sort.

I must admit I did go through another victim phase, where I thought: Why me? Why am I not like other people? Others don't breakout when they gossip. Why can't I have clear skin like others? But I had no choice other than to accept what I was experiencing, as the more annoyed I became, the more havoc I'd create in my body.

I recall Oprah once saying that God speaks to you firstly through a whisper, then a nudge, a hunch, and eventually a brick wall. It really was true, my Source had always told me to follow that better feeling because when I engaged in gossip (or any form of negativity towards others), I didn't feel good inside. I had just learnt to shut that voice up, and so the signs were becoming more and more obvious. This was my wall, except it felt more like getting run over by a truck on a daily basis. So I made a conscious decision to avoid negative conversations permanently.

Then within a matter of weeks something amazing began to happen. People around me (friends, colleagues, family members) who were most in harmony with the gossip I no longer wanted to be a part of, began to leave my experience one by one. Colleagues left my team for new positions outside the company, those friends became busy and communication was reduced, while my family member's behaviour started to change. It was amazing. As soon as I decided I no longer wanted that toxic energy in my life, people and circumstances began to change to accommodate my new energy. I didn't take any physical action, I just decided to cut the gossip and focus on seeing the good in myself and other people. It's nothing short of amazing to see the way the Universe orchestrates events and scenarios for you, to meet your new desires and emotional state.

Milk it!

During the rest of 2011 I learnt to divert my attention to positive things and appreciate even the smallest occurrences. I would milk as much joy as I could from my work, my family, my alone time, the thought of my niece (who was not even born yet), the sunshine outside every morning when I woke up, the bus that took me to work, my colleagues, literally everything. I would think of creative ways to make every task enjoyable during the day. For example, I never liked grocery shopping, but it had to get done, so I started thinking of my trip to the grocer as a culinary excursion. I'd imagine all the wonderful cheeses and multi-grained organic breads I would find at my local wholefoods store, or the delicious dark chocolates I would come home with. And within a few minutes, I was excited about getting groceries and couldn't wait to get in my car. The advantage of setting yourself up with good expectations of anything is not just the fact that you feel good immediately, but also the creative influence you will have on your reality. The more you expect good things, the more you attract what matches your good feeling expectations. I played many of these games with myself in order to sustain a good feeling state and allow my body to rejuvenate and heal itself. And my body healed very well. By the end of 2011, there was no evidence of back or hip pain, and very few skin problems.

Of course I'm human and still had moments of not so elevated emotions. And I've learnt that it's okay. I've learnt to make peace with where I am at any point in time, and know that the future will be different. The future will match my new thoughts and emotions, so there is no need to stress about it.

While you have a specific issue (health-related or not), if you take a more general look at your life, you'll find that overall things are going well for you. This can often be the key to your recovery. Recognising that you are generally doing well will give you hope for the future and also make the present less uncomfortable.

"You were born with wings, why
prefer to crawl through life?"

—Rumi

PART 2

Feeling Your Way To Healing

In part 1 of this book I went into the details of my quest for wellbeing and how the more I tried to take action to heal my body, the more illness I attracted. In part 2, I will share how I used the LOA to attract wellbeing. I have seen too many examples of the LOA working in my life to doubt its existence any more. Once you wake up to the presence of this law, many of your life-long questions get answered.

In writing this book, my intention is to empower people so that they may heal themselves. I think of myself as a student in the classroom of life and I want to share my notes with fellow peers. I have spent many years studying and researching the subject, so I hope the principles in this book will allow you to take a shortcut to your destination. I will share with you useful information necessary to kick-start your wellness.

I have also listed further reading and viewing materials at the end of this book, and I highly recommend you continue your path of self-discovery by studying the works of the many amazing teachers out there.

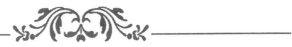

"Everything in the universe is within you. Ask all from yourself."

—Rumi

CHAPTER 3

You Are A Walking Magnet

There is a law called the Law of Attraction (LOA) that is and has always been present. Whether you know about it or not, you are under the influence of LOA, just like you are under the influence of gravity. Gravity acts regardless of whether you know about its existence or not. It is for this reason that it's in your best interest to understand how LOA works and use it effectively in your life. There is great leverage in using this law to your advantage as you will soon see.

Through the release of the book *The Secret,* a lot of people heard of LOA for the first time. This book, however, only touched the surface and as a consequence, many people did not see sufficient results. I read the book in 2006 and did experience some success, although very small. After not seeing sufficient progress in my life, I continued my search and found the source of much of the material to be the teachings of Abraham by Esther and Jerry Hicks. Since then I have continued my research and found other teachers around the world discussing it with different semantics. Some approach the subject from a religious context, while others are a more scientific.

My introduction to Abraham

When my first Abraham book arrived (*The Law of Attraction: The Basics of the Teachings of Abraham*), I was so excited. I could feel this was the type of book I would finish in one sitting. I couldn't wait to devour all the knowledge that could potentially change my life. At this stage I did not know that Abraham was not one person, but a group of consciousness from the non-physical dimension channelled by Esther Hicks. And frankly, as soon as I found out that minor detail, I was really creeped out. In fact, I was so uncomfortable with the idea of channelling, ghosts or anything non-physical, the book went straight onto my bookshelf. I needed time to digest what I had just read. And the book sat there for many weeks until I finally made a decision to pick it up again. I decided that I had nothing to lose by reading it. Regardless of who the authors were, if it could be of benefit to me then it was worth reading. And I could always give it away if I didn't see any results. Going forward you will notice Abraham being referred to in plural, because they refer to themselves as a group of loving entities. So I started to read, re-read and more importantly, apply their teachings in my daily life.

While I didn't understand all of the material, most of the practices were incredibly useful, especially Segment Intending. I began using Segment Intending every day, and achieved some amazing successes in my professional relationships with managers and co-workers. Later in this chapter; I will explain how I personally practise Segment Intending.

The more I applied their teachings, the more abundance I was able to manifest and the more interested I became. But it wasn't until I attended an Abraham Hicks conference in Sydney where I got to watch the incredible manner in which Abraham speaks through Esther Hicks that I really understood that Abraham is infinite intelligence. There were thousands of people in the audience with raised hands, eager to ask their own unique questions. But there was not enough time in one day to have every question asked. Yet Abraham was able to intelligently answer the questions of a few people in such a way that everyone else's questions were also answered. I certainly had all my questions answered, without having to ask any. Watching Abraham live really helped solidify their love and intelligence in my eyes.

So if you have problem with channelling, as I did, here are some tips from Abraham themselves:

> "You could leave the channelling out of it. Call it inspiration; that's all it is. You don't call the basketball player a channeller, but he is; he's an extension of Source Energy. You don't call the surgeon a channeller, but he is. You don't call the musician, the magnificent master musician, you don't call him a channeller, but he is. He's channelling the broader essence of who he is into the specifics of what he is about." (Abraham-Hicks.com.)

Going forward, I will refer to the universal creative force as Consciousness, Source Energy or just Source. It is what I am most comfortable with. You may like to refer to this energy as God, Allah, Universe, Spirit, Essence, Inner Being, insert-whatever-you-like-here. It is really up to you and I would recommend you stick with whatever connotation feels better.

The Law of Attraction

The LOA states that like attracts like. What you put out with your thoughts (and emotions) draws to you matching manifestations (with identical energy). This is where proverbs such as 'what you give is what you get' stem from. The give part, however, is always energetic despite common knowledge. Furthermore, there is only inclusion in this Universe. There is no concept of exclusion in the realms of the LOA, which is always acting, always present. I know we have all been taught exclusion by society; we have been taught that saying 'no' to something is the way to prevent it coming into our experience. But this is a misunderstanding of how things really work.

No means Yes

One of the most important concepts to get your head around is the fact that our world is a inclusive world, meaning you cannot exclude anything. Our concept of exclusion is based on a lack of knowledge about how things really work, and a distortion by society. You have been taught by well-meaning people that saying 'no' to anything unwanted will prevent it from happening. And saying 'yes' will invite it into your experience. But this is actually incorrect, because it is not your words that shape your reality but your thoughts (powered by emotions). What you pay attention to (fuelled by emotion) is drawn into your life, not what you say yes or no to. And the stronger the emotions behind your focus, the greater pull power you have.

Think about it in this way. At any point in time you are only thinking about one subject. You get to choose if it's a wanted subject or an unwanted one. By paying attention to something, you are inviting it (or something of a similar energy) into your experience. So in other words, by constantly giving your attention and focus to what you do want there is no possibility for what you don't want coming into your experience. Similarly, by giving your attention to what you do not want, even when you clearly don't want it, you are activating that thought vibration in your experience. And if this vibration is kept active long enough, it will manifest into a physical life experience you can see, hear, smell, taste or touch. It's important to know that in order to heal, your thoughts need to be on wanted instead of unwanted subjects, most of the time. As a matter of fact, in order to allow any other wanted manifestations into your life, most of your focus must be on the wanted.

Conversely, give your predominant attention to unwanted things and watch as unwanted manifestations pop up in your life.

Think about your own life and you will undoubtedly see many examples of this. The harder you try to save a relationship, the quicker it falls apart. The more you try to please your boss, the worse things get at work. The more annoyed you feel during the day, the more annoying people and experiences fill your day. And in my case, the more I tried to 'heal' my body, the more illnesses I discovered and the worse I got.

Pay attention to people around you and you will see it occur vividly. How are the lives of those most negative turning out? I have noticed those who generally complain a lot find more and more situations about which to complain. And it's not that these people are making it up, things really do turn out bad for them. They are just not aware that it's their own focus causing the attraction of more like vibration problems.

On the contrary, we have all seen people who have stayed focused on what they wanted succeed in life with very little effort. It's interesting that society often labels them as selfish, when all they are doing is following their inner guidance. I have seen this in every area of life, and it is especially true in health. I have friends who live unhealthy lifestyles (by current medical standards), yet are always at their optimum weight and incredibly healthy. While I myself have experienced the opposite, I did everything by the book, ate quality foods, exercised, had my all my regular checks, and spent big on health professionals, yet my condition continued to deteriorate.

Does this mean if I keep thinking about having a car accident, I will attract it? Not necessarily. You may attract a car accident or a series of other experiences that will be on the same vibrational level to your thought about the car accident.

The vibrational nature of thoughts

Before we go any further I must explain thoughts and their properties. Your brain is a transmitter and receiver of thoughts (hence thought vibrations). Every thought you have ever thought has had a wavelength and frequency. Each wavelength/frequency combination of a thought determines the emotion you evoke in yourself. For example: when I think of my baby niece, I am filled with love and appreciation for her. But when I think of a past partner who has hurt me, I feel anxious instantly. Higher frequency thought vibrations (faster waves with a shorter wavelength) feel good. Lower frequency thought vibrations (slower waves and longer wavelength) feel bad. So the better you feel, the higher your emitted vibrations and the worse you feel the lower your emitted vibrations.

In Diagram 1 I have sketched what a high frequency vibration, evoked by the feeling of love, looks like in comparison to a lower frequency vibration, evoked by fear.

Whatever vibrations you emit (and you are always emitting vibrations) you will receive back in the form of physical manifestations. So the unhappier you are, the lower and slower your emitted vibrations, resulting in more things to be unhappy about. This is consistent with the illnesses I experienced during unhappy phases in my life, and the wellbeing I started to experience as I became happier. It seems to be consistent with the experiences of those diagnosed with cancer. Before the cancer ever existed, something was the cause of great unhappiness in these people. And often they were unhappy for such a long time before being diagnosed with a disease, that they themselves didn't connect the dots. It may sound a bit too simple at first, and it actually is quite straightforward once you become more sensitive to how you're feeling. The more conscious you become of your feelings (good or bad) the more you will see examples of the world around you reflecting back the result of your thoughts and emotions.

Love = Fast High Frequency Waves

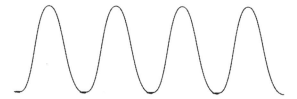

Fear = Slow Low Frequency Waves

Diagram 1 – Love and Fear vibrations

Thought vibrations (backed by emotions) have pull power, they are magnetic. You are literally a walking magnet and are drawing to yourself experiences and manifestations (unknowingly) that are in harmony with your vibrations. What have you been attracting into your life experience so far?

Your magnetic fields

Your brain has a strong magnetic field, being a strong transmitter and receiver of thought energy. As you start to understand the power of your brain and hence your thoughts, your desire to stay focused on what you want will increase, making it easier to manifest the healing (or anything else) you want. The interesting thing is that the magnetic field of the brain, while very strong is miniscule compared to the magnetic field of the heart. Scientists have discovered that our heart's magnetic field is 5,000 times more powerful than our brain's magnetic field. This is why your emotions play a bigger role in your manifestations than your thoughts or words alone.

Just like any engine requires fuel to power it, thoughts require strong emotion in order to have strength or pulling power. Your heart is a powerhouse of electromagnetic energy and combined with your thoughts, has the power to create amazing miracles in your life. Society today puts so much emphasis on the power of the brain but has completely ignored the heart and its role in creating our reality.

> "The heart generates the body's most powerful and most extensive rhythmic electromagnetic field. Compared to the electromagnetic field produced by the brain, the electrical component of the heart's field is about 60 times greater in amplitude, and permeates every cell in the body. The magnetic component is approximately 5000 times stronger than the brain's magnetic field and can be detected several feet away from the body with sensitive magnetometers." (Rollin McCraty n.d.)

The speed of consciousness

It's important to share some interesting research into the speed of consciousness. All around the world scientists are researching the subject of consciousness and I believe the models from Dr William Tiller are extremely eye opening. He explains that consciousness cannot be blocked by any barrier, including lead and mountains of rock, which are normally capable of blocking even the highest frequencies of electromagnetic rays (ie Gamma rays). So his theory is that consciousness must therefore be of a higher frequency than the Gamma rays spectrum, to allow it to penetrate these barriers. In other words consciousness must travel faster than the speed of light. How much faster?

Dr Tiller's model has multiple dimensions:

Level 1—Second Chakra (Sacral) can send consciousness as coherent information at the speed of 34.7 billion miles per second.

Level 2—Heart Chakra can send consciousness as coherent information at the speed of 64.64 quadrillion miles per second.

Level 3—Consciousness emanating from the Crown chakra is sent at the speed of 2.5 million light years in a fraction of a second.

So if within seconds our consciousness can travel to other galaxies, imagine what impact it has on your physical body here and now?

You are the most POWERFUL and FASTEST energy transmitter.

Your BRAIN + HEART = ENERGY TRANSMITTER and RECEIVER. Whatever frequency you emit, the same frequency is drawn back to you through a MAGNETIC pull. This is probably why we have always heard statements such as 'what goes around comes around'. Yet the true meaning behind these statements has been lost, and they have been interpreted too literally. We have all been in situations where we have been very giving in a friendship or relationship, and it has not been returned. And the real reason lies in the fact that it's not your actions but your vibrations that have this magnetic pull. Your thought vibrations determine what you get in life, regardless of how it may appear on the surface.

Thoughts vs. Words

During the years of studying the works of various teachers I came across many who insisted that you be careful what words you use. Many of them put great emphasis on avoiding negation and never using 'not' or 'no' because if you say 'I do not want to be fat' the message heard by the Universe is 'I want to be fat'. So I spent a lot of my time earlier on in my journey double-checking everything I was going to say, which was a nightmare. Or after the words came out, I felt like I had to correct them. It was impossible to do. Luckily it turns out that this teaching is not entirely true, these teachers have omitted the most important factor, which is your emotional state. Your predominant emotional state governs how things turn out in your life, and all the sentence correction in the world will not make a difference. In mathematics the greater than (>) symbol is used to imply 'more than'. Therefore:

Emotions > Thoughts > Words

In other words, your emotions play a greater role than thoughts alone, and thoughts play a greater role than words. It doesn't matter if you say you don't want X or you do want Y. It is your underlying emotion that determines the outcome, not the words you use. You could use happy positive words about a subject, but feel miserable towards it and the outcome of your experience will reflect your overall feelings.

Getting back to the power of thoughts, as soon as you give your focus to anything, your brain transmits a vibration, which begins to attract more similar vibrations to what you just emitted. Those vibrations that begin to be drawn to you result in events, situations, people who have a similar vibration. This is why we hear comments such as 'birds of a feather flock together'. This is why wealthy people are surrounded by other wealthy people. Abraham says that this is also why doctors and scientists who are busy studying disease keep finding more and more evidence of the disease, and rarely rendezvous with cases where the disease has been healed by so-called 'miracles'. We tend to label an unexplained healing as a miracle, simply because we do not understand the mechanism by which it happened. At some point in the future when there is a scientific reason for the healing, the label of miracle will be removed.

A real example from my life: When I moved into my new home, my well-meaning family started telling me how it was unsafe, could be broken into easily and that I should never have purchased it. While I felt good purchasing it at the time, listening to other people caused me to doubt my decision. Within a few months I felt like I needed to protect myself, purchased insurance in case something went terribly wrong, changed all the locks—just in case—and even started researching security camera options.

I was not sensitive enough to the way I felt to realise I was emitting vibrations of vulnerability and insecurity. That vibration (emitted for well over a year) combined with the expectations of my family resulted in my home being broken into. Initially I thought it came out of the blue. How could this happen to me? My privacy was invaded, my personal belongings taken and I felt totally vulnerable. Yet after about five weeks of thinking it through, I realised the incident was triggered by my negative emotional state during the four weeks prior to the break-in. While I had been influenced into feeling insecure about my home by those around me all along, nothing had gone wrong over the previous year. Then one month before the robbery I had opened my home to an acquaintance who needed a place to stay for four weeks. One week into her stay, I found out she had taken the liberty to go through my personal belongings while I was at work. This had made me absolutely furious, I felt taken advantage of by someone I had trusted, my privacy was totally invaded. I even wondered if she had stolen anything. Then one week after she left, my home was broken into and I lost some of my most valuable belongings.

In retrospect this incident taught me a lot about being sensitive to the way I feel and not letting myself feel negative. I learnt that **your vibration depending on the length of time and intensity of your emotions, in combination with your expectations, is released into the Universe and begins to draw to you more scenarios and**

situations to validate your initial feelings. Then a year later you are robbed and you think it came out of the blue. Of course you did not want to attract a break-in, no one does. But the LOA acts on your emitted vibrations constantly, whether you realise it or not.

The negative feelings I felt during that time also had consequences on my body. My immune system was weakened and my hormones went crazy. It took another month for me to raise my emotional state again, yet when I did, I was in a much happier place than before the break-in. I took the bounce. It's actually very important that you clean up any old vibrations or thoughts you may have about a subject, because if you don't, they may still manifest like my situation reflected. Abraham's Focus Wheel technique is the best way I have found to do this, and I'll discuss it a little later.

It's like the Universe is constantly reminding you that you are a creator of your life situation, not a victim. And the better you become at paying attention to these reminders, the quicker you are able to take your power back.

A real example from my life: After switching from a very stable steady paid job to one that I was passionate about but had no experience in, my best friend and I got talking about the redundancies that had happened the previous year in my first company A. Also, only recently some of my colleagues in company B had been retrenched. At that stage I was enjoying my new position at company B, however I knew that due to the global financial crisis, many companies were making many redundant. My friend (out of her own worries about her current situation) then asked: 'What if they make you redundant? What if you lose your job? What would you do?' The discussions went on for about an hour, and I kept replying that I'd be fine no matter what happens. I didn't want to introduce that unsure vibration into my own life, but at the same time, the more I defended myself against the questions, the more unsure I felt. Of course she meant no harm and was merely feeling unsure herself and searching for clarity. But over the next few weeks, I thought about conversation more and more. The more I thought, the more insecure I felt about my new job at company B.

A month later I was made redundant. I managed to attract exactly that which I didn't want. I remember having mixed feelings about it. I was both unsure of where or when I'd find work doing what I loved again, while another part of me felt like I'd be okay regardless. I certainly handled the redundancy better than another girl who broke down as she was told she was being let go. The interesting thing was this girl was still living at home, rent free and had no responsibilities or bills, while I was in a very different financial situation. But I remained hopeful, I still believed things would turn out okay for me, even though I could see no evidence at the time. And the different mindset between myself and this other girl is what led me to better work immediately (I was unemployed for exactly one day) while it took her a few months to find employment.

So why did this happen to me? I now fully understand that I attracted the redundancy the second I started feeling unsure during my conversations with my friend. But the fact that she brought the subject up in the first place also indicates that I must have had this active in my vibration well in advance. So not wanting to lose my job was more active in me than wanting steady employment (with this employer). And as with everything else that happens in life, I really do believe things work out for you perfectly if you allow them to. I went on to land my dream job in another company, which has paid off tremendously both financially and professionally for me. Perhaps if it wasn't for the redundancy I would still be in company B with less pay and would not be as happy as I am now. But the biggest lesson in it for me was how consistently the LOA works if you pay enough attention.

"Your ease or disease are symptoms of
the balance of your thoughts"

—Abraham Hicks,
CD 1, Special Subjects Series

How disease is attracted

When I first explain to someone that we are all creators of our experience, including our health, I find they ask: "Why would anyone attract disease to themselves?" Often they have had a loved one suffer from cancer or other severe ailment. So I want to clarify this point. No one attracts a disease by thinking about that disease too much. No one likes the thought of disease, so the chances of someone thinking about it enough to attract it are very slim. No one would choose illness over wellness, poverty over abundance. But we do unknowingly attract disease to ourselves by becoming a match to the vibration of that disease.

We are huge vibrators of energy, we are magnets made of consciousness, flesh and blood, but unfortunately society has put its focus on the flesh and blood component and completely ignored the metaphysical and vibrational aspect of humans. When I've spoken to people who have had loved ones pass away from cancer, after asking questions about the patient's emotional state before the cancer was found, they have always admitted that the patient was unhappy for a long time before cancer was found. The cancer survivors I've spoken to have also confirmed that in retrospect there were strong negative emotions present before the diagnoses.

It makes sense from a physical point of view. Prolonged negative emotions weaken your immune system, making you susceptible to potential diseases. Depending on the length and strength of the negative emotions being experienced, the body experiences a vast array of problems such as acute respiratory diseases, metabolic disorders, high blood pressure, ulcers, rheumatoid arthritis, and so on. There is a strong link between our emotional state and our body's healing ability.

From a metaphysical perspective your body's natural ability to repair and heal itself is blocked by negative emotions. Remove the negative feelings and your cells begin to heal immediately. Of course it could take some time before you see the physical manifestations, which is why Abraham has always advised not to take score of your progress too quickly. If you do this (usually when the body hasn't yet shown enough evidence of healing), you will lose hope. And losing hope for healing is enough to make your condition worse. What you should take score of is your emotions, and this is the only thing you need to know if you are on the path to wellness or illness. Abraham refers to this as your Emotional Guidance System. This is your Source or Consciousness guiding you towards more joy, happiness and abundance and everything else you have wanted all your life.

A real example from my life: As soon as I have a thought about my newborn niece whom I adore, the good feelings I am showered with are my indicators that I am heading towards wellness (and joy in every aspect of my life). Conversely, as soon as I remember that bill that has just arrived, which is substantially larger than I expected, the negative feeling in my stomach is an indicator of my blocking wellness.

At this point of becoming more aware of my feelings, if I chose to continue down that negative path, more like vibrating events are drawn to me. I may encounter less-than pleasant people, I may attract a parking ticket (which highlights the feeling of lack of abundance), or I may feel discomfort in my body. The physical discomfort I personally feel is actually a blessing because it lets me know immediately that I am off track. Whereas when things went wrong outside of me, I did not initially accept I was attracting them. Usually we blame other people for anything outside our body. The car accident was the other driver's fault, the parking ticket was the councils fault, the computer failure must be a faulty software, etc. But for me bodily conditions were strong reminders of how aligned my thoughts were to what I wanted.

"Reason is powerless in the expression of Love"

—Rumi

The power of love

Our body is a biofeedback mechanism for our emotions. You do not just get sick by accident or bad luck. Unknowingly you have created the ideal environment in your body in which the disease was able to develop and thrive in. Our bodies are like ecosystems that can house all sorts of illnesses if the conditions permit. Conversely, our bodies also contain amazing self-healing abilities, and healing will take place if conditions allow.

Dr Glen Rein has found the DNA heals itself in the presence of loving energy sent intentionally (to direct the heart field). Intention is necessary to give the heart field energy direction (towards an organ, cell or biochemical pathway). "In this way our thoughts and intentions can manifest in the body at the biochemical level bringing about actual physiological changes associated with the healing process." (Glen Rein 1996)

Think about that for a moment. If love is the emotion that our DNA resonates with most, then doesn't that mean we were born to love? And any feeling less than that means our cells are not functioning at their optimum capacity. You are slowing your body's ability to heal itself or find its own balance when you accept your physical condition is a consequence of genetics, or the environment, or whatever label the medical industry has given you. Choose now to become a creator of your own reality. It is so much more empowering than to be a helpless victim.

"Natural atomic and molecular vibrations in the body emit
EM and acoustic energy fields which regulate biochemical
processes thereby manifesting as health or disease."

~ Glen Rein, Ph.D. Biological Effects of Scalar Acoustic
Energy: Modulation of DNA, 1998

Know that when you have loving thoughts about someone, they will receive them. Regardless of their location or proximity, they will feel your vibrations. They could be on the other side of the planet, your loving thoughts about them will be received and felt.

The HeartMath institute has proven that one person's heart signal can effect another's brainwaves, because love is not just an emotion but an electromagnetic phenomenon. (Linda Marks 2003)

But why do we need science to prove it? Haven't you ever thought of a good friend and had them call you? I have many relatives overseas. The ones I am closest to emotionally and love dearly either call or email me within a few hours of me thinking about them. Or when I call them, they admit they were thinking of me. It happens all the time if you pay close attention.

Because humans are mostly comprised of water it makes sense to look at the influence of love (the highest emotion) on water, which we depend on for survival. The power of emotions on water crystals has been photographed by Dr Masaru Emoto through his groundbreaking research, and has had enormous impact on my own perception of this life-giving resource.

The research showed the effect of loving and hateful thoughts on water crystals (Masaru Emoto 2010). Water crystals exposed to 'Thank you' formed beautiful snow-white symmetric shapes, while water crystals exposed to 'You disgust me' disintegrated into discoloured random blob-like shapes. This is yet another example of the power of emotions on the matter not just around us but inside us. If positive thought about a simple glass of water has this influence on the water crystals outside us, imagine what loving thoughts will produce inside your body. We really are far more magnificent than we know.

Recognise your resistance

When you have a bad experience, in that moment you experience contrast. You realise what you don't want and ultimately what you do want. If you focus your attention on what you don't want, how you could prevent it from happening again, why bad things happen to you or whatever negative trail of thoughts you happen to choose, you introduce discord in your vibration.

Abraham refers to this as resistance, and the way to recognise the resistance is your feeling during a thought. Every thought has a feeling, and as you become more sensitive to your feelings, you will begin to recognise negative feelings quickly, before they lead to physical illness. Physiological problems in your body are just the result of negative thoughts (or resistance) that have been ignored for far too long.

It took me a few years to really understand that my bodily state follows my emotional state and has nothing to do with my diet or lifestyle choices other than my thoughts and emotions. With every negative thought I have, Source begins to disagree with me, leading to discord within my body. Because your body is the closest thing to you, resistance is often displayed in your physical state before your relationships and finances, although not always. Some examples of resistance for me include the gut-wrenching feeling I get when I try hard to make a relationship work, or when I desperately want to get a boss's approval, to be liked by a popular group of people. It just doesn't feel right, and your instincts always tell you. Your Source knows you don't need approval from others and that you have been created worthy.

Feelings could be subtle

Depending on how much you have listened to your Source or instincts or gut feelings to this day, you may find initially that it's not immediately apparent to you how you are feeling about a subject when it enters your mind. But don't worry, and don't try to analyse every thought you have. Just relax and make it your intention to feel better throughout your day. As you set this intention (and therefore transmit its vibration), the Universe will orchestrate events around you so that you do feel better. I know this for sure as, whenever I start my day with this clear intention, my day unfolds beautifully.

Just decide right now that you want to see more things that make you feel good, and as you give your attention to more positive occurrences through your day, you will begin to experience more to feel good about. It's a cycle, which is why we often see the rich get richer and the poor get poorer. It is your emotions and hence your vibrations bringing you life experiences, not your actions. Think of yourself as a walking magnet, which you really are. When you feel good you attract good feeling situations, people and events. Or vice versa. Decide right now what you want more of in your life, and give it your positive attention.

Fork Off!

One of the techniques I have found very useful in raising my thought vibrations has been to fork off in the direction of what I want when I notice what I don't want. Abraham teaches that there is immense benefit in noticing what you don't want, because it provides the contrast necessary to allow you to know what you do want. In any moment when you notice something unpleasant or unwanted, you realise what you prefer instead. The trick is then to turn your attention to the wanted subject, and ignore the unwanted. This is called forking off and I have found it extremely beneficial in staying focused on my desires.

The challenge for most humans is the focusing of the mind on what is wanted instead of the unwanted. We have been taught by society to take the unwanted event, person, circumstance and apply as much action and time against it to turn it into what is wanted. Yet this accomplishes the opposite, as our attention to the unwanted always creates more unwanted in our life. Looking at my past, the more illnesses I tried to fix by correct medication, diet and lifestyle changes, the more I found to fix.

For example, when your employer is unpleasant towards you, instead of thinking about how unpleasant it is to deal with him or her, focus your attention on what you want, which is a better more pleasant employer. And as you focus more on what is wanted, you will see life around you change, so that either your employer becomes more pleasant, or you interact with him or her less when they are having a bad day. And eventually either you will always run into them on a good feeling day, or you will soon be drawn to a new team or company with a pleasant employer. Or in my case, the manager leaves and is replaced by someone lovely to work with.

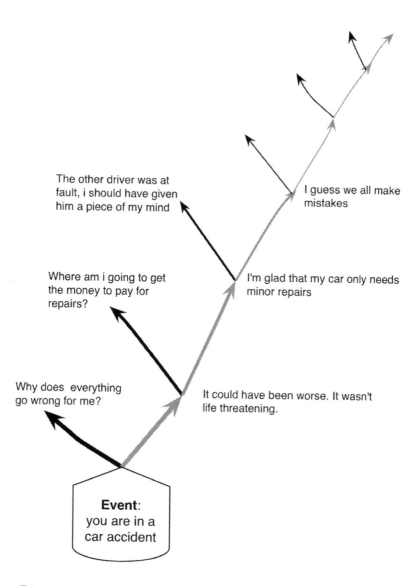

Diagram 2 – Forking off in the direction of better feeling thoughts

"The only reason for time is so that
everything doesn't happen at once."

—Albert Einstein

Use the time delay

As you begin to see that your health can return and the body you want can be yours, the next logical question is when? It's totally natural to want everything now, and the last thing you want to be is patient. However, your current physical condition didn't just happen overnight. A lot of negative thoughts and emotions went into creating the illnesses in your body. And so a certain amount of positive thought and emotion is needed to allow your body to recover. Therefore you'll find a time delay between your practising of good feeling thoughts and your body displaying any improvements. The good news is that this time delay is a fraction of the time it took to develop the physical condition in the first place. You will find relief in knowing that just because you had a condition for ten years doesn't mean it will take another ten years to heal. Your wellness is far greater than you know so a little effort in feeling better and caring about your feelings will go a long way to repair your cells. The delay will not be very long, provided you don't doubt or question your improvements. I highly recommend you use this time delay to focus more on what you want, and really shape and design your thoughts into the best versions of your desires, so that when they manifest you can be sure to love the manifestations. Use this time to iron out any wrinkles in your thoughts or expectations about what is coming to you, it is the perfect opportunity to really think about what you want.

In my experience, the raging back and hip pain with which I lived for five years took a couple of weeks to disappear, although they'd reappear any time I felt negative enough. So the time delay was really very short. But my hormonal imbalances that I had for about thirteen years took about two years to resolve themselves. During these healing years, even though I was well aware of the remaining conditions in my body, I kept my focus on what was going well for me (my family and career) because I didn't want to slow my progress down any more. As a consequence, while my body was balancing, my career took off and my relationship with my family strengthened.

What I want you to take away from this section is: **Relax and enjoy yourself, your body is healing on the inside even though you may not see evidence of it yet. Divert your attention to what is working well for you, and before long your body will give you more and more reasons to feel good.**

Acknowledge your blessings

It's important to acknowledge even the smallest signs of joy around you. Use even small incidents to make yourself feel better, play up every positive occurrence in your life as much as possible, however small. Appreciate everything that is going well for you at the moment and you will see a momentum begin, where you notice more and more things to appreciate. Look for goodness around you and then appreciate it. Use your imagination as much as possible to spot goodness if you must. Try to assume the best about people and circumstances, and you will always get the best out of them.

A real example from my life: Years ago I was stuck in a rut at work and really unhappy with the manager I had to report to every day. I had felt for a long time he was treating me unfairly and giving me the worst projects possible, while my other colleagues were given the best opportunities. I had clearly seen what I did not want in this manager every single day, for many months. Noticing what I did not want meant thinking about what I did want in a manager. But it wasn't until I started focusing more on what I did want that things began to change for me. I remember one afternoon when I had reached my limit with him, I went into a quiet room and thought to myself that I would no longer give my attention and focus to him and the way he was treating me. In that moment I became very clear about what I wanted. For the first time the majority of my focus was on the wanted subject, not the unwanted one. I left the room, returned to my desk and did nothing else physically. I didn't take any action, I didn't try talking to him, I didn't start looking for a new job. But for the next three days, I felt differently. I no longer felt like a victim, I had taken my power back. On the fourth day, the company announced his resignation. A month later he was replaced with a really wonderful manager who I loved reporting to. The clarity I had gained as a consequence of the first manager had led to me attracting a much better manager, who ticked all the right boxes. This experience not only taught me the power of my thoughts and feelings, but also reminded me of the massive influence we have in shaping our own reality.

Appreciation > Gratitude

Did you know that appreciation is actually better than gratitude? I learnt from Abraham that there is a difference between the vibrations of gratitude and appreciation. What you want to get to is appreciation; it has a higher vibration and better feeling. Appreciation is the closest feeling to the feeling of love, which is the highest emotion one can experience. I personally feel that with gratitude there is a sense of settling for what is, a feeling of "I'm going to be grateful for what I have, even though it's not much". It's almost like there is a motive behind the feeling. But when I appreciate something, there is no feeling of limitation, only a feeling of love for what I am appreciating. It's like 100% of your attention and focus is on the subject of your appreciation, which is why it feels so exhilarating to appreciate. If you are finding it hard to appreciate anything, then at least be grateful for what is going well in your life. Gratitude might be where you are at right now, which is perfectly fine. Begin where you are and keep moving forward to greater feelings by choosing better feeling thoughts.

Creation = Energy (99%) + Action (1%)

Abraham has always said that 99% of creation happens in thought and thought form before it is manifested. The last 1% of manifestation comes about through inspired physical action, but its creation by Consciousness is the first 99%. In terms of my body and its health, the way I have come to understand all this is that I am 99% metaphysical and only 1% physical (body, flesh, bone). So my health has far more to do with my emotional state (and the vibrations I constantly emit) than my diet or exercise program. And the evidence speaks for itself. As soon as I feel happier and sustain that newly-raised emotional state long enough, my body heals more rapidly, my skin clears, my flexibility and strength increases. My blocked nose dissipates almost immediately. My headache stops suddenly, my hip pain disappears, and so on. This is despite me making no changes to my diet or lifestyle. But as soon as I become sadder (for whatever reason) and it continues for a little while, my body starts to show discord very quickly. Illness is your body's way of disagreeing with your emotional state. So I know very clearly that this is the key to health (or anything else you want) in life. You must first get your emotions raised (which equates to 99% of the creation), and that last 1% comes to you through what they call inspired action. Someone suddenly brings up a solution to a health problem you had never discussed. You bump into people who are of great benefit to your health. You turn on the radio and the subject you're thinking about is being discussed. Or like me, you get emailed an answer to a problem you noticed a week earlier, but didn't worry much about.

A real example from my life: After practising Abraham's teachings and becoming more aligned with my bigger metaphysical self, I stopped trying so hard to make things happen. I had a blood test in 2011 and the doctor found normal levels of estrogen and testosterone but extra androgens floating around. While I wasn't pleased about the extra androgens, I was happy to have normal levels of the other hormones. As I walked out of the doctor's room, I briefly thought to myself: Wouldn't it be nice to have less androgens? I wonder how that could be achieved? But my attention was placed on something else almost immediately after that and I forgot about the whole thing. Two days later I received an email from a newsletter subscription labelled "Spearmint reduces Androgen levels in Women", and I thought Wow! What a weird coincidence, I was just thinking about this the other day. The interesting thing was, this subscription website is a general information website and is certainly not focused on diet or wellbeing, let alone female hormones. So I took this as a sign from the Universe and really appreciated it. I then did my own research on the subject and found that it has proven successful for many women, and decided to try it. While I knew it wasn't a permanent solution to my problem, I felt grateful for being shown a temporary solution while I continued to heal internally. And it certainly was not a coincidence. I asked the Universe, and I was answered very quickly. On the contrary, if I had become obsessed with finding a solution to the problem, and taken action before the energy was ready, chances are I wouldn't have found the solution to my problem and probably attracted more health concerns in the process, like I had historically. Instead I asked "Wouldn't it be nice?" without desperation or neediness. I gladly took the spearmint tea for four months until I felt my body no longer needed any help from the outside. In other words my faith had become strong enough after seeing more and more examples of wellbeing in my life that I began to believe everything was okay with my hormones. Yet still I hesitated getting another blood test, because I knew taking score too soon could backfire. A year later my test results showed that not only had my testosterone fallen even more than before, but the androgens were also a thing of the past. I was so happy, I skipped all the way home that day.

In the first part of this book I have described how much money and time I spent taking action in trying to resolve my health issues. All this did was create more health problems for me to try and fix, because my focus was on the illness, not wellness. It is a law that no one can budge. Then as soon as I stopped trying to fix it all (as I had tried and got nowhere fast), and put my focus on doing things that felt good to me (painting, relaxing, seeing friends), my body began to heal. And yours will too.

Exercise 1: Love List

Get a notebook you love and on one page, write the numbers 1 to 10 down the page. Make sure you love this notebook, search a few days if you must to find something that is special to you. Next to each number, list anything that you love right now about your life. It could be your puppy, your partner, your salary, the novel you just started reading. I don't care what you list, as long as you feel some appreciation for it. Throughout your day look out for things to take home and add to your love list. For me it might be the smile of a toddler or the way the wind blows my hair as I walk to work. Nothing is too small to be listed here. Try and fill in a page per day, and within a few weeks you will have listed hundreds of things that evoked appreciation within you. The purpose of this practice is to get you into the habit of looking for lovely things. Not only do you feel better when your focus is on good feeling thoughts, but you will begin to see more good coming into your life.

Exercise 2: Appreciation Journal

In another notebook (or the same), list what you appreciate about the people in your life. At the top of each page, add one name, and fill the rest of the page with what you appreciate about that person. It is always easier to do this with those you already like. If you are having a hard time with someone in your life, list some other qualities about them that you appreciate. She may have never treated you well, but she may have a great sense of style. Perhaps she is a successful businesswoman even though she sucks as a boss. I know it's really hard to list anything about people who have hurt you, but what you will find is that as you begin to list their good qualities, you will begin to have better experiences with them. The point of this exercise isn't to keep people you don't want, in your life. On the contrary, it's to help you release them from your experience and bring more of what you do want. My intention is to get you into the habit of noticing more good qualities in others, which ultimately result in pleasant experiences with them. As I began to notice my colleagues' good qualities, I also began to attract more and more good experiences with others at work. Over the next few months, you will not only be amazed at how much your life has improved but you will also start to really appreciate your own ability to manifest in your life experiences. I also think you should add your own name to the top of the page once in a while and get into the habit of listing things you appreciate about yourself. The more you add to your journal, the more good things you will notice in your life. This is the reason why in so many religions we are reminded to give thanks and be grateful. Because when you turn your attention to what is working in your life, your body begins to find relief from the tension brought on by the original thoughts that created the illness (or whatever problem you have).

Exercise 3: Wouldn't it be nice if . . . ?

Abraham has taught me the power of this simple statement when wanting something. When you ask "wouldn't it be nice if [your request]?" you are not asking from a place of neediness or desperation. You are not trying hard to make anything happen. It's a light and playful way of thinking about what you want, without introducing discord or resistance in yourself. I recommend you try it out for yourself. Walk around looking for what you want, and what would make you feel good to have in your life. Then instead of saying 'I want a relationship, I want a healthy body, I want . . .' replace your statement with something softer like, Wouldn't it be nice to meet the perfect partner? Wouldn't it be nice to have a new car? Wouldn't it be nice to get promoted?

Exercise 4: Go to sleep happy

When you go to sleep feeling good, you will wake up in the same good-feeling place. Similarly going to bed unhappy means you will wake up tomorrow in the same mood, which effectively sets you up for a not-so-great day. So what you should do as you begin to prepare for bed is start appreciating anything that is easy to appreciate. I like to lie in bed and appreciate my luxurious bed linin, my soft pillow, my supportive mattress. It doesn't matter what you appreciate, as long as you fall asleep feeling good, because I guarantee you will wake up in the same mood. Then the positive momentum you wake up with will carry you through the day.

This simple practise made a huge difference in my life and really aided my body's ability to heal itself. As I practised thinking happy thoughts at bed time, I found my sleeping patterns improved. I'd fall asleep very quickly and wake up every day re-energised. I also like to sleep to the Abraham Hicks Guided Meditation CDs playing softly in the background. While these guided meditations are intended for you to meditate to, I have found them very effective even to sleep to as Abraham's vibration and voice tends to sooth you to sleep.

Exercise 5: Segment Intending

This technique of Abraham is incredibly effective because it allows you to focus on a small segment of your day and set your intentions ahead of time. You can decide how small or large your daily segments are, but I break my day up by activities. During the week my segments consist of: Preparing for my day, travelling to work, work (which

I usually break into smaller segments), travelling home from work, preparing dinner . . . And for each individual segment I set a clear intention (or two) ahead of time. For example, as I awake and get out of bed, my intention is to enjoy my breakfast and dress professionally. As I leave the house and start walking to the train, I declare how much I appreciate the train service that gets me to work in a timely manner and I intend an enjoyable journey. During my day, especially before meeting with various stakeholders, I go over my intentions again with myself. I visualise the outcome of the meeting and remind myself what I'd like to achieve from my meetings. Segment Intending has been incredibly useful for me professionally and has led to many successes. I must, however, point out that in every meeting I went to I had spent days if not weeks prior to that meeting, truly appreciating the people I worked with. In other words, you can Segment Intend all you want. If you are not resonating positive energy about people or, worse, you are resentful towards people, your chances of manifesting what you want are small. Once again we arrive at the absolute importance of feeling appreciation and love.

Exercise 6: Focus Wheel

Abraham Hicks's Focus Wheel is the best technique I know for cleaning up your vibrations about any subject. Not only does any remaining negativity about a subject get ironed out, but this technique helps raise your vibrations to a new place. The more you do it, the better you feel and the quicker things change in your life. It did however take me about eight Focus Wheels to get the hang of it, so be patient with yourself. I apply this technique by drawing the following diagram on a large piece of paper, numbering each pie or sector from 1 to 12, like a clock.

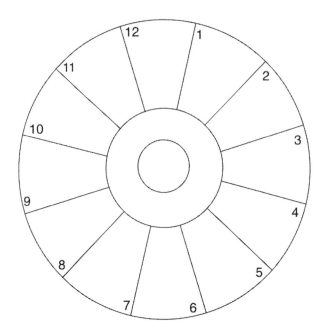

Diagram 3 – Abraham Hicks Focus Wheel

Start by writing your desire in the inner circle. What is it that you really want? Usually when we want something we have resistance to, there is a tension inside us. For example you may want to wear a bikini this coming summer, but none of your previous attempts at shaping up for a bikini have been successful. So while the desire is there, the belief is not strong. The best metaphor for the Focus Wheel is a children's merry-go-round. The merry-go-round must slow down in order for you to get on. And the way to slow it down is by thinking of less-resistant thoughts about your desire. Start by thinking of a thought about your current bodily state and write it into sector 12. This thought must not be too far away from where your current emotional state is (on the subject of your body image), or the merry-go-round cannot slow down enough for you to get on. If the wheel is spinning too fast, trying to get on results in you being thrown into the bushes, so to speak. So you must get on the wheel gently, by finding better—and nicer-feeling thoughts about your body, to write down in each sector. As you search for and write down better-feeling statements, you are cleaning up your vibration on the subject (and effectively raising your emotional set point). By the time you get to sector 11, you should already be feeling much better about your object of desire. This better-feeling is the most important indicator you have, it guides you in the right direction. After finishing sector 11, finish the wheel by formulating one final and best feeling statement about your subject of desire. Write it in the outer circle. Depending on how you feel about any subject in your life, you will have to complete a number of Focus Wheels before feeling any release and seeing any changes in your life. Don't, however, make it a task for yourself. Only do these exercises if it feels good or you will hinder your progress. Here is an example of a completed Focus Wheel:

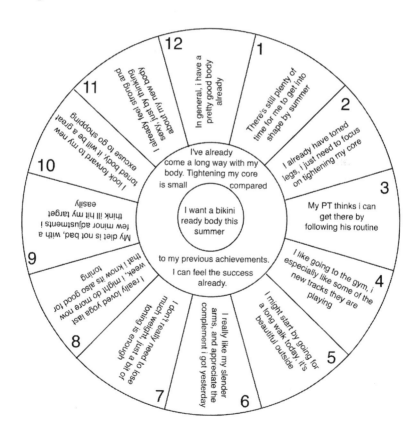

Diagram 4 – Sample Focus Wheel

Exercise 7: Let's see what I can evoke today?

In one talk, Abraham suggested saying to yourself "let's see what I can evoke from you today?" to the people in your life. Once I tried it out I was amazed at the results. While I had started to slowly come to terms with my influence in my own reality, the idea wasn't 100% solid for me. There was a colleague who sat opposite me every day, who I felt acted a little awkward towards me. I wasn't sure why as I knew he wasn't shy. He was quite talkative with other colleagues, I just wasn't sure why he never initiated any conversation with me. So one day while I was listening to music and feeling good on the way to work, I said to myself, "I wonder what I will evoke from him today?" not really expecting much but curious enough to try it out. I walked towards my desk, placed my handbag down and before I had even had a chance to look up he said in a friendly manner, "Hi, how are you? How was your weekend?" I was totally surprised because, to be honest, I wasn't really expecting anything to change so quickly.

Out of surprise I said, "Really well, how was yours?" once again not expecting much conversation past that point. Then he proceeded to tell me about his son's birthday party in amazing detail. This guy who had not spoken to me for months while sitting meters away was telling me about his family and weekend. Amazing.

So why don't you try it? Start your day by saying to yourself "I wonder what I can evoke from people today?" Then, as you attract good or bad, you become more conscious of your own part in the way things play out for you. It's really quite incredible.

"Any malady in your physical body was a lot longer in coming than it takes to release it."

—Abraham Hicks

Excerpt from the workshop in Napa, CA on Thursday, February 27th, 1997

CHAPTER 4

LOA and Health

Your current physical state is temporary, so don't stress yourself into feeling worse as that slows down your recovery. It's temporary, therefore ease yourself into a better-feeling place. Make an effort to think in the direction of what makes you feel better. Does the thought of your leg recovering feel better? Does the thought of your back pain resolving feel better? Keep turning towards a better-feeling state. You may have to put on rose-coloured glasses for a while and ignore the present situation until it changes. The sooner you take your attention away from what's bothering you and give attention to something that makes you feel joyous, the sooner you will deactivate the negative vibration that has been bringing the health issues into your experience.

Every time you think and feel, you are affecting the vibrational state of your body. **If your thoughts feel good, then the result is good vibrations through your body. Your thoughts affect your body, whether you know they do or not. Choose better-feeling thoughts.** Negative thoughts and emotions effectively de-harmonise the vibrational state of your cells and organs, resulting in illness.

Avoid talking to other people about your health issues. I know it may seem like a good idea. You may think they could have a solution to your long-standing chronic illness. But talking about something you don't want (even if it was an accident that you experienced in the past) strengthens that vibration in your present. The LOA in turn will bring more similar events and situations that match this vibration. For me it was almost like a game I would play in my mind, to see how long I could go on avoiding the subject of my health problems. People couldn't understand why I didn't want to mention I had a health condition, so I'd pretend I didn't have the condition as much as possible. The game I played was to see how long I could avoid the subject that day.

As you start to get happy and see the results, you will begin to see the massive power of your emotions and how important they are in your life. Your emotions are here to guide you towards your highest good. No one except you has the ability to know where you stand regarding any subject, and hence how you feel at any moment in time. You are therefore unique and precious.

I recall Abraham saying 70% of creation is complete before you begin to feel hopeful about it. And 99% of creation is complete before you begin to see evidence of it. If you feel hopeful about something, it's almost created for you. **Hopeful is a strong indication that you are almost at your destination.** But if you feel sad or, worse, depressed about your body's condition, that's an indication that you are not close to healing. You need to make this an emotional journey instead of a physical one. It's how you feel, right now in the midst of the arthritis, back pain, breast cancer or whatever else is going on in your body that matters. Do you feel hopeful? Do you believe there is a way and you will find it? You must find a way of separating what's happening right now from how you currently feel. I accomplished this by reminding myself that my current life was a consequence of my past thoughts and energies. And this made it easier for me to believe in a better future, as I knew my present thoughts and emotions are much healthier than what they were in the past.

We are all on a different emotional set point for each subject in our lives. So while you could be depressed at work, you may be content in romantic relationships. As long as you're going upwards in the emotional scale on all or any subjects, you're making good progress towards your desires. You need to know that if you feel angry over subject X, it may be because you were previously depressed on that subject. That doesn't mean you are not hopeful in other subjects. But your anger on that one subject is an indication that you're reaching for better-feeling thoughts and moving up towards better-feeling emotions. While others may not like your anger, you have still made progress. Abraham has always taught that a rise in your emotional state will mean moving into anger from depression, and this is a good thing. You are taking back your power, and while society around you may not like your new found anger, you are still heading in the right direction. The next diagram is The Emotional Guidance Scale from Abraham. Have a look at it and think about where you are on the subjects of money, health, relationships. As you care more and more about the way you feel, you will begin to move up on the scale and life will unfold in tremendous ways for you. And usually your body will display the first evidence of your new emotional state

The Emotional Guidance Scale

1. Joy/Appreciation/Empowered/Freedom/Love
2. Passion
3. Enthusiasm/Eagerness/Happiness
4. Positive Expectation/Belief
5. Optimism
6. Hopefulness
7. Contentment
8. Boredom
9. Pessimism
10. Frustration/Irritation/Impatience
11. Overwhelment
12. Disappointment
13. Doubt
14. Worry
15. Blame
16. Discouragement
17. Anger
18. Revenge
19. Hatred/Rage
20. Jealousy
21. Insecurity/Guilt/Unworthiness
22. Fear/Grief/Depression/Despair/Powerlessness

As long as you are moving up the scale, you are heading in the direction of health, vitality and abundance in every subject you desire. The reality is, if you are currently depressed about your situation, you cannot make a sudden jump to joy, it's not possible. I tried and failed. But as I started to feel better (by focusing on things that felt better to me at the time), I began to go up the emotional scale steadily. Some people may reach revenge, which I now understand is better than depression. I felt angry at all the doctors and specialists selling me expensive products that were undermining my wellbeing. And as I started to go up the emotional scale, my anger was replaced with hope for healing. At the time I didn't know that the anger was just a phase I was going through on my way to hope and then love. So just keep going up and up. It is okay to feel whatever you are feeling now, but focus your attention from now on to what you do want, and as you focus on the wanted subject, things will begin to shift in your life and health. Have a look at the Emotional Guidance Scale and think about where you may be on that scale, on any subject in your life. Remember with every subject, you will be in a different place. For example while I was unhappy with my doctors and parents for not finding a better solution to my hormonal problems when they first arose, I was feeling quite content financially. I had a good job that paid me very well, so on that subject my emotional set point was much higher.

"When you do things from your soul,
you feel a river moving in you, a joy."

—Rumi

CHAPTER 5

Your Only Task: Get Happy

When you think about what you want, it is always because you believe you will feel good by reaching your desire. Your purpose of wanting anything is the feel-good end result you are expecting. So the 'what' and 'why' are always clear in your mind. And because of this clarity about what you want and why you want it, your energy is aligned (or lined up with your desires). Therefore you instinctively feel good when you think about the 'what' and 'why' of a desire.

On the other hand, when you start thinking about the 'how' or 'when', is it going to ever happen? How long will it take? When will it happen? How can you find the right people and resources? How will you get from point A to point B? your energy alignment is often lost.

We don't usually have the answers for the 'how' or 'when' component of a desire until a while later, once there has been sufficient thought about the 'what and 'why'. This is why, when you start thinking about the 'how' and 'when' prematurely, you instantly feel negative emotion, call it doubt, worry, fear, anxiety. When you ask questions you don't have answers to, you are not heading towards your desires manifesting, which is why you immediately feel a drop in your emotions.

74

It's for this reason Abraham advises you stay focused on the good feeling end result of what you want, instead of putting your focus on how to make it happen. **It is not your job to figure out the "how".** The Universe will pull you in the right direction, you will see things revealed to you bit-by-bit like a puzzle when you follow your good feelings. Good emotion is the Universe's way of showing you the right path. While your physical mind does not have the foresight to know where you are going, your higher mind does. Your higher mind can see far in advance and knows what is the quickest most enjoyable path to getting you to your destination. Your higher mind communicates with you using your emotional guidance system, through feelings. Good feelings mean you are heading in the direction of your desires. Bad feelings mean you are slowing down your momentum towards your desires. It seems so simple, yet we need to be constantly reminded.

This was a big lesson for me as I was always such an action-oriented person. I believed I had to work hard to achieve anything and spent years trying through action to heal my body. I thought you must set goals for anything you want, and make plans to take steps towards them happening. But all I did was get in my own way. This was such a resistance-inducing method as I spent more time on the 'how' than on the 'what' and 'why'. No wonder I was getting sicker and sicker.

So, as this chapter name implies, your only task is to get happier, starting now. Make it your intention to find more and more things to feel happy about, and your focus will be drawn in that direction as the Universe starts to bring together all the components needed for your desire to manifest. Plus it's much easier and much more fun to enjoy your journey to wellness, wouldn't you agree?

Once I began to care about feeling good, all the missing pieces of the puzzle came together. Coming into alignment and loving myself was like a homecoming. It reminds me of the song *Coming Home*, with the lyrics "they've forgiven my mistakes". Your body really does forgive your misalignment as soon as you start to love yourself.

Don't let your judgement of me or these teachings stop you from making great progress. And don't assume I'm wrong or accept what I say. Just test what I'm suggesting and see the results for yourself. Give it a try. Words don't teach, you must try it yourself and see. With what you now know, you cannot go back to not knowing your own power in the creation of your experience.

"Ignore those that make you fearful
and sad, that degrade you back towards
disease and death."

—Rumi

Treat yourself with care

During this time of healing, I recommend you surround yourself with positive people and things. Watch more comedy, and movies with positive happy outcomes. Avoid watching anything that is not uplifting and not joyous. Avoid any horrors or thrillers. Avoid most of the media if possible and don't watch the news, don't read the paper, remove yourself from the anxiety that you are being fed on a daily basis. The majority of the news is negative, and will hinder your progress by focusing your attention on negativity (lowering your emotional state). Making these changes will give you a better chance at returning to your happy state and will speed up your recovery. And remember, unless you are well yourself, you have nothing to give your loved ones. So your happiness should be your number one priority.

Talk about any good news you hear and focus more on finding things to feel good about. When you give your attention to the media, you are being distracted from the creative amazing person you really are. You are disconnecting from your Source a little. You should be spending as much time uplifting yourself as possible, your wellbeing depends on it. As you make it your intention to get happy, negative people will leave your life naturally, you won't need to take action to make it happen.

Look for more examples of people who have successfully healed themselves. There are many out there, and you will begin to hear about them as you make it your intention. Ask the Universe to give you more examples of people who have had progress in their lives. For me, that inspirational person was Louise Hay, I knew she had healed her cancer, so I knew my conditions could also be healed.

Don't forgive, if you don't want to

It seems almost all religions and spiritual teachings encourage forgiving as a critical step towards healing. And it is true, that until you are able to let go of your emotional and psychological attachments to people and events in your past, you won't move forward with your life.

> "To forgive is to set a prisoner free and discover that the prisoner was you."

> ~ Lewis B. Smedes

I first tried to forgive because of the various teachings out there preaching its importance. And I must admit forgiving took some time. Depending on how deep the wound is, it sometimes takes years to forgive and ultimately forget. Forgiving and forgetting go hand in hand, I don't believe you can really forget without forgiving first. And despite some saying 'I have forgiven but not forgotten', if you have not forgotten, then that's a really big indicator that you have not fully forgiven. But how do we forgive people who have really hurt and betrayed us? Louise said it best:

> "We may not know how to forgive, and we may not want to forgive; but the very fact we say we are willing to forgive begins the healing practice."

> ~ Louise Hay

Often the simple act of deciding you want to forgive (or do anything else for that matter) begins the process in your life. Forgiveness allows you to free yourself from the limitations and shackles of someone or something from your past. The quote **"holding resentment is like eating poison and waiting for the other person to kneel over"** is spot on.

So if you are holding any grudges against anyone, forgiveness is certainly an important step towards healing your emotional wounds and scars. But in my personal experience and the experience of those closest to me, forgiveness can only take you so far. I have recognised that forgiving seems to only partly help heal our wounds from the past. After spending years and years trying to forgive people from my past, I still felt like a victim.

I still felt that in trying to forgive other people, I was at some level admitting to being a victim to someone else's wrong doing. And the more sensitive I became to my feelings the better I was able to feel such subtle feelings I was having towards the traditional forgiveness approach. So for a while I stopped trying to forgive. Instead I focused on what made me feel better and began to see how much my emotional state influences my daily life and manifestations. And as I gained more of an understanding of my own power in my life, I started to see people as just instruments for delivering to me what I had sent out vibrationally. People and my experiences with them were just mirroring my emotional states at any single point in time. And that's when the lightbulb finally switched on.

I came to the conclusion that there was actually no one to forgive, as I had only been receiving the essence of that which I had been transmitting outward. All those years of being bullied at school were a reflection of how bad I felt myself (and continued to feel). All the rotten rascals that had hurt me could not be any different, considering how unlovable I felt. And later, all those wonderful people who have come into my life and brought me joy were also reflections of my internal state, my thoughts and, ultimately, my emotions.

And that is when I was able to truly move forward with my life and forget the past, when I realised I am actually the powerful creator of my experiences. When you just go about your life reacting to everything based on the way it made you feel and not giving much notice to feeling good, you are creating by default. It's basically operating in auto-pilot mode. This person was bad, so now I feel bad. This person was good so now I feel good.

But the place you want to reach is called deliberate creation. It's when you choose what thoughts to focus on based on how it feels to you. And as you choose better and better-feeling thoughts, your Source Energy guides you to better and better experiences, where you realise you are no longer just reacting to everything around you, but are a deliberate creator of your own reality. This is the best place to be because you know no matter what happens, no matter what your government, wife, husband, boss, child does, you know how to feel good. This knowing is so powerful and gives you such stability that you begin to thrive in any environment, regardless of what is happening around you. And as you move to better and better experiences, you begin to see the powerful Being you are and always were. It then becomes very clear to you, the role you have unknowingly played in your past negative experiences.

And that is when you can really take your healing to a whole new level. When you realise your role in your past experiences, you are effectively taking your power back from all those people who have hurt you, which effectively cancels the need to forgive, **as you realise there is no one to forgive. The people who hurt you were simply reflecting back to you, your vibrational state.** They were simply devices and tools by which the wonderful Universe around you brought to you your vibrational match. You unknowingly gave your power to them, by thinking you were a victim.

I cannot describe how satisfying it feels to finally come to this understanding that all the past was my own doing, and so my future can be the way I want it to be. It doesn't get any better than this.

My advice is first try to forgive (if you haven't done so yet). Pay close attention to how it feels. How does it make you feel? Do you feel relief? If so, keep going down the forgiveness path. But if, like many, forgiveness does not feel like relief, leave it alone. For a while stop thinking about whoever it is you need to forgive, but instead focus on finding thoughts that make you feel good. And as you feel better and better, you will see your life get better and better, to the point where you begin to understand the role you play in your own reality. As this understanding strengthens, you will start to feel less of a need to forgive anyone, as other people become irrelevant. Your new-found perspective of the world will make people from your past less and less significant to the point where there is nothing left to forgive. All forgiveness is, really, is you taking your focus from something that bothers you and putting it on something that feels better. It lets you get relief.

Making peace with what is

An important teaching from Abraham is to make peace with what is. Accept that you are where you are, but still have hope for a better future. Making peace with where you are means you trust life to take care of you, you trust the process and are willing to allow it. If you are not able to make peace with what is, it's very difficult to clean up your vibration enough to manifest anything different in the future. This doesn't mean you should condone problems in your life, it just means you don't beat yourself up over anything you are living, now that you've realised it was you who attracted it.

If I had not been able to make peace with the fact that my pain would return or my skin would breakout every time I felt negative, I would not be able to appreciate the awareness I have gained as a consequence of this journey. It took me about a year to truly feel grateful that my body is guiding me in this way. I now appreciate the fact that my body reminds me every time I am off track. I'm certainly no saint and it's taken time for me to get to a place where I feel no resentment about it. I think the real reason why my body had to show me I was off track in such a drastic way is because I had been ignoring my inner guidance for such a long time. I had learnt to shut that inner voice that would tell me not to criticise someone right before I did it. We are all born with this inner guidance, and some of us shut it down with food, drugs and toxic thoughts.

As you begin to listen to this inner voice, it will become more frequent and louder, guiding you more and more towards wellbeing. Similarly, as you ignore your inner voice, the reminders become bigger and bigger until you can't deny it any more. While in some people the reminders are manifested in the form of disease, in others it's financial or relationship troubles.

Just be gentle with yourself, we all make mistakes, it's part of the process of learning something new. What you are now learning is self-love, which I promise you is the best possible medicine for your body.

Retracing or reverse healing

During the healing process your body often heals in reverse, so if your illnesses began in the order of illness A, illness B and illness C, often C heals first, then B and then A. When deep healing is occurring, sometimes you may experience old symptoms from the past re-appearing. All this, however, depends on your level of resistance, which you can reduce by elevating your emotional state. It's far easier to get happy and stay happy, to allow your cells to heal rapidly, than to spend thought energy focusing on your symptoms to try to figure out why you are experiencing a health condition. This is exactly how my illnesses healed over time, and the next sketch is a visual representation of how this reverse healing happens.

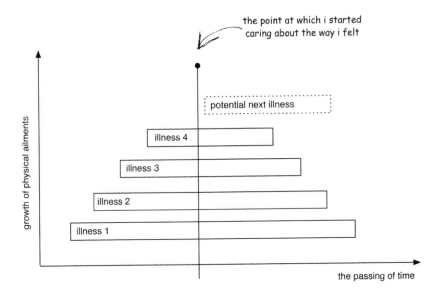

Diagram 5: Reverse healing of illnesses over time

Recurrences

On the subject of being human, and forgetting to keep my emotions elevated, I have to mention that any time I forget and go back to my old ways of focusing on what I don't want and trying to fix problems by fighting them and pushing against them, the breakouts begin and my hip pain returns. Or I may suddenly start sneezing and coughing, as if a cold has set in from nowhere. These are just fast indicators of discord that appear in my body. For you it could be very different. The indicators of the resistance you have introduced in your life could be in the form of headaches, arthritis, heart disease, broken bones, turbulent relationships, critical managers, accidents, financial trouble, the list goes on. The severity of the indicators always matches the severity of your resistance.

A real example from my life: We all have certain topics in our lives that are more sensitive than others, and in my life that topic was the theft of my mother's inheritance by two of her siblings. In 2011 I'd have many months of great health, great skin and vibrant body. Then I would attend a family gathering where the topic of my mother's inheritance would be brought up, and I'd be filled with anger and frustration over the injustice. While my annoyance was valid, it was ultimately not good for me or my loved ones. If I'm not operating at my optimal, there is very little I can provide those around me.

By giving my focus to what I didn't want (my mother being taken advantage of), I was disconnecting my own wellbeing, because my Source (or my metaphysical self) is only ever focused on wellbeing. My Source only focuses on wellbeing and me not doing the same, results in negative emotions. So overnight a sharp shooting pain returned to my hip and my face was covered in large cystic acne. This happened twice in 2011. The first time it occurred I promised myself I'd never let it happen again.

The second and last time this happened I was so angry at myself for letting myself get upset (over something I could not do anything about) again, that I broke down in tears in front of my family. They were all shocked as it was the first time they had ever seen me cry as an adult, but I just couldn't stop. The sobbing was uncontrollable and I remember feeling sorry for myself, for carrying all this anger and stress in my body and spending the past few years paying the price. That was probably my lowest point in a long time. Plus I felt a little embarrassed for crying like a child, having not shown a tear for the majority of my life to the people I am closest to. But there was another feeling present, a feeling of immense release and peace. I knew from then onwards that I would never feel that angry again. I would never let something else take precedence over my wellbeing. I would never let other people's actions take away my happiness. I realised then that I am the most important person in my life, and until I feel good, I have nothing to give anyone else.

These tears were a form of release, and I must have let go of a lot of resistance on that night because I bounced back to my happy self the next day. And this time there were no breakouts or hip pain, because the strong resistance (anger) had been released for good. I was far happier and more joyous from that point onwards than before. My vibration had risen considerably as a consequence of that night.

And the subject that had bothered me so much for years no longer created an emotional reaction in me. I had effectively cleaned up my vibrations regarding that subject. This same process of vibrational clean up happened a number of times manually by doing Focus Wheels. As mentioned earlier, through the process of the Focus Wheel, you can clean up your vibrations (thoughts) on any subject of your choosing in the privacy of your home. I've used this technique many times and I would recommend it to everyone.

Clean up your vibrations before it gets bad

It is now time to free yourself from this prison of illness you have created unknowingly so that you can start to live the good life you were born to live. As you watch your body heal, you will begin to understand the true power of your conscious mind, which you may have been unaware of until now. Get started on cleaning up your vibrations and replacing them with higher frequency thoughts. As I iron out the wrinkles in my own vibrations (that's how I imagine it) on not just the subject of health, but money, family and relationships, my life begins to flow more easily. It is amazing how quickly results start to show around you. Your life is a mirror, a reflection of your inner state. If what you see is not pleasing, you cannot blame the mirror. You must change in order for the reflection to change. I suggest you get into the habit of not letting negative vibrations build up but instead clean up your vibrations with a few Focus Wheels per week. Be open to the possibility of things changing for you, and they will.

CHAPTER 6

The Other Stuff: Medicine, Diet and Lifestyle

Why I avoid medication

Once again I am not dispensing medical advice, only sharing what I know from my own experience. Based on research and my own experiences, modern medicine does not really heal your body. Apart from the effects it has on the brain (and your emotions), medication sometimes also acts against the body's natural processes towards healing itself. On a physiological level, when you take a cold and flu tablet to stop the runny nose, you are not allowing your body to rid itself of the bacteria it has ingested. The runny nose is your body's way of detoxing.

But more importantly, from an emotional level, the cold (or whatever the physical imbalance) is your body's way of telling you that you are not in vibrational harmony. Negative thoughts lead to negative feelings, which when ignored long enough, cause discord. The illness is an indicator that you are not focusing on what you want (and ultimately not feeling good). I personally try to avoid any form of medication as much as possible, and prefer to see signs from my body as gentle reminders that I have not been taking care of my feelings. I understand that the more severe and painful the illness you're experiencing is, the more challenging it becomes to focus on good feeling thoughts. Sometimes it seems impossible to find a good feeling thought, and in those situations, the easiest way to find relief (and take your focus off the problem) is to divert your attention to something else. You need to find some way of distracting yourself from what's currently bothering you, and one way I found effective was watching comedy. Laughter is a fast way of releasing resistance and tension, emotionally as well as physically. Whatever subject you choose to give your focus to, make sure it feels good. I have learnt to appreciate the signs of discord in my body, because they are like a tap on the shoulder, a subtle reminder to stay on track with my thoughts and emotions. I truly believe modern medicine buys you time, not health. It buys you time so that you may change your emotions and allow real healing to take place inside you. You cannot make your health someone else's problem. It is unfair to expect your physicians to fix you. You are setting yourself up for disappointment and it's a load no physician can possibly carry.

A real example from my life: In mid 2010 my right calf developed a red itchy rash. It was just one of my many symptoms of discord, but at that stage I was under the impression that I could do something about it physically. I thought I could take 'action'. So I tried a number of herbal rubs, I replaced my toiletries with organic products, I even took a few homeopathic remedies for it. Nothing helped and over the next eight months, it grew from a 1-inch diameter to a 4-inch diameter. By then it was time to move homes, and as I got busy with the move my focus was taken off my health issues (one of which was the rash) and put on the organisation of the removalists and logistics. And one day, about two months after moving into my new place, I remembered there used to be a rash on my leg. A rash that was now gone, and not a trace of it remained. The move had preoccupied me so much that my chronic back pain disappeared, my skin started clearing and my rash disappeared.

Before you throw out the pills . . .

While I point out the truth behind modern medicine, there is still a place for it. Modern medicine works well in emergencies and acute situations where the patient needs relief from severe pain. If you are on medication for a serious condition, don't suddenly stop the medication. The reason for your illness is your emotional state, and your emotional state is also your solution.

Abraham has always advised that we must continue the action journey as we have been for a while, but now focus on the emotional journey. The medication gives you stability, making it possible to focus on raising your emotional state to allow deeper healing to take place. If you suddenly stop the medication (depending on the severity of your condition) before having raised your vibration enough (and sustained it long enough), your physical condition could get worse. The important factor in your healing is your state of joy, and as you spend more and more time feeling joyous, your body will show signs of healing. And as your health begins to improve, you can work with your doctor to reduce or stop the medication.

In your metaphysical body, you have received the healing. The healing you asked for, when you asked for it, was given to you. It's just that your physical body has not caught up with it because your negative emotions got or get in the way. Instead make your whole focus feeling better and raising your emotions up the scale.

For a while you may have to pretend (if it makes you feel better) that the healthy body you want has come. For me it was a pretend game. When people asked me how I was, I'd say I was well, even though I had a sharp pain in my hip every step I took. I was stubborn and just refused to give in and give up. I refused to return to the specialist after promising to never go back. Being persistent pushed me to keep searching for the solution, and while at the time I didn't know how my negative emotions had created the condition, I felt that an optimistic outlook would help me get out of the hole I was in.

Take an emotional journey

Thus you must first go on an emotional journey as Abraham advises, and sustain that newly-found emotional state before your body starts to recover. Once your body has recovered sufficiently, you can then, in consultation with your doctor, reduce the treatments or medications.

The danger in stopping your medication and treatments before you heal emotionally is that your body may not yet have the emotional stability to allow its true recovery, and you could cause more harm than good.

Go on the emotional journey first and watch as your body starts to thrive. You will start to feel so good that your happiness will eventually become the drug that will take you forward to new levels of wellbeing.

But be aware that there will be a lag time between where you are emotionally, and where your body is physically. For a while your body may still appear ill even though you yourself feel much better emotionally. This lag time could be days, weeks or months, depending on the length of time you had the negative emotions that led to the disease in the first place.

Don't let this lag time disappoint you into thinking you have not made progress. You have and are making great progress in healing; it just takes a little time for your cells to renew themselves. This recovery time also depends on your expectations and beliefs about your condition and ability to heal. The Universe will give you fast recovery if you expect it. For me, the severe back and hip pain that I had had for about five years started to fade within two weeks. I had a very strong desire for healing, and believed it was possible, because I could still remember a time when I didn't have such raging pains in my body.

Resistance is always going to show itself to you, whether through your body, in your relationships or another area of your life. Keep an eye out and as you start to feel better, you will also notice other aspects of your life get better.

Although I am emotionally better than ever before, if I go back to the negative thoughts, my body will very quickly show its disagreement. Even to this day, if I try to push against anything, if I criticise someone, if I gossip, I will be greeted with a pimple the very same day. As annoying as this is, I am able to look at the benefit it has for me by reminding me when I'm focused in opposition to what my Source is focused on.

What thought feels better to you?

Think back to when you were a kid, full of excitement about the world. Your imagination would run wild without any hesitations about what others thought. It's over time that society beats that out of us, and we begin to conform. We begin to assume our bodies must decline with age, because it's happening to everyone else around us. Now take your imagination and pretend for a while that things are going well for you, that your bodily future can be different and things can change. Refuse to be told otherwise by any negative people around you. No disease has more power over you than your own thoughts. How strong is your desire to go forward and overcome your illness? You must persist with believing the healing is happening.

There are many great doctors and specialists doing what they can (based on their training) to bring health to patients. However, each one of them could look at you, the patient, and conclude a different diagnosis based on their own background, training, history, culture and experiences. Only one person can give you a true perspective of your condition and that is you. You have the true perspective because only you know what is going on in your heart and mind at any one time, so you cannot turn to someone outside you for opinions. I learnt this the hard way, and while I know words do not teach, I hope you keep this in the back of your mind the next time your doctor gives you a diagnosis. Doctors have been trained to expect illness because that's what they see all day long. After all, no one visits them out of wellness. Therefore, when a doctor looks at you and diagnoses you with a medical condition, decide for yourself who you choose to believe. Does it feel better to believe there is no cure? Or does it feel better to think of the condition of your physical state as only temporary? As you begin to look for better-feeling thoughts, you will see more reasons to feel better. The more reasons you have to feel better, the quicker you see evidence of your body's wellbeing. And gradually your beliefs begin to change.

This is the period of time when you need to wear the rose-coloured glasses and act as if the healing has already happened or has at least begun. It may seem like you are fooling yourself and I happily refer to it as you're delusional phase. The healing is taking place but because the evidence is not yet there, your doctors or family members may think you are a tad delusional. But that's okay, persevere anyway. It's not these people trying to recover, so their attitude to your wellbeing should not take priority over your own.

Negative emotions block your body's ability to protect itself. But when you are happy, your vibration is higher, and enhanced healing is able to take place to the point where you will not notice any sickness to begin with. For example, you consume a virus, your immune system immediately begins working to balance your body, and because you are well emotionally, your body heals without you even becoming aware that there was ever a problem in the first place.

But when your vibrations are lower (due to negative feelings), you prevent your body's cells from recovering. So while your cells have asked Source for wellbeing, you are in the way of them receiving it.

Conversely, as soon as you realise you're sick or unwell, all it takes is for you to raise your vibrations by getting happier and sustaining that emotional state long enough for your body to recover fully.

I have found this is the best way to avoid catching bugs at work during cold and flu season. Working for a large company means I share amenities, and interact with, hundreds of people. Sometimes a variety of viruses are present in our offices. I've certainly seen a direct correlation between the strength of my immune system and my general happiness. There have been times when the majority of our department has been ill, and I've not caught anything, while at other times when rarely anyone is sick, I will catch one cold after another for 'no apparent reason'. Of course now I know the cause very well and it's all my emotions.

Don't go back to negative ways

If after recovery you go back to your old ways of unhappiness, then the same illness or something that matches your vibration will return to you. I've had so many ups and downs on my journey to full recovery that I now know for certain that it is my emotional state guiding my body, and everything else in my life for that matter. I have just been fortunate enough to realise this at a relatively young age, before the diseases became more disabling or life-threatening.

I have no doubt that if I had continued down the path of unhappiness my many symptoms would have continued to multiply and bring me more unhappiness.

So I am forever grateful for the tough years I had for they have brought me to such awareness of my spirit and body connection. It's funny, talking about spirit, because I never perceived myself as a spiritual person. I actually remember in my teens telling my family that there is nothing spiritual about me!

I appreciate great physicians

I have to acknowledge the exceptional health professionals (like my chiropractor and acupuncturist) that I crossed paths with on this journey. These people understand our emotional state plays a huge role in our body's physical state. While they may not know the vibrational nature of thoughts, a good health professional should take a more holistic approach to helping you heal. When you do turn to a physician, ensure they don't just view you as flesh and blood.

While I have much respect for homeopathy, and still recommend it to others, I must point out that an external vibrational remedy cannot fight the vibrations you constantly emit with your thoughts and emotions. If you would like to try homeopathy, wait until you have managed to get a handle on your emotional state and have started to raise your emotional set point. This applies to any other form of medicine for that matter. You could consume the best foods and medicine in the world but still create havoc in your body just by thinking incorrectly.

Take the path of least resistance

One of the biggest factors in your recovery is taking the path of least resistance. It really goes hand-in-hand with feeling good, because some times you may be in situations where taking the path of least resistance is the only way to feel good. While I have mentioned throughout this book my stance towards using modern medicine for health, I must also explain that sometimes modern medicine is the path of least resistance. Some people with cancer often have doctors and family members insist that they go through chemotherapy, while they personally do not want to. This disagreement about the best method of treatment will create immense discord in the patient. It is always best to let the patient decide for themselves what feels like the best path to take.

You may be in a situation where taking the path of least resistance means agreeing to the method of treatment that your doctor, partner or family strongly support. If you feel much more discord and resistance by not listening to them, then you are better off taking the path of least resistance by following their advice. It is really something each person must decide for themself, it's a personal decision as no one else is inside you feeling for you. What feels like the right decision?

A real example from my life: With the birth of my niece early in 2013, I was asked by my brother and sister in-law to have certain vaccinations, just in case there is a dormant virus that could be passed on to the baby. With what I know now about the LOA and our immense wellbeing, I knew very well that there was no chance of my niece becoming ill and I also believed in my own wellbeing. However, I knew also that the rest of my family have much faith in vaccinations, and my not getting the vaccination would result in immense arguments among us as a family. And chances are they would feel so worried that their worries alone would probably create more health concerns in the new infant than anything else. So in this situation, I took the path of least resistance, and got vaccinated. Not doing so would not be worth the trouble and turbulence in our family, so it was just easier to get vaccinated even though I believed in my own wellbeing as well as the baby's.

"You wander from room to room
hunting for the diamond necklace that
is already around your neck"

—Rumi

Diet with alignment vs. diet without alignment

Today we are constantly told what to eat and what to avoid by the media, scientists and medical professionals. A little while later some new discovery is made about the potential dangers of the same food we were told to eat previously, and the confusion increases when the diet you always had must now suddenly be avoided. If eating a healthy diet is really what leads to good health, then why does the same diet not bring health to everyone? Why is it that no one diet works for everyone?

When I first heard from Abraham that our diet plays very little role in our health, I was a little surprised. I thought, then is someone who eats fast food as healthy as someone who eats only organic, carefully prepared meals? It took some time for me to get my head around this concept, especially because I had been taught from a young age that fast food is bad and should be avoided, while all meals must be highly natural and home cooked. But after my unsuccessful detox and my dietary changes in the attempt to regain my health, I started seeing that Abraham is correct.

It is not the food itself that brings us health, but our emotional state. If I am in a good state emotionally, it seems nothing I eat harms my body. I have certainly seen this when it comes to the subject of weight. The only times I have gained weight were times of great depression. Yet as I get more joyous and spend more time in a higher emotional state, the weight just falls off, no matter what I eat. And boy do I eat!

So does this mean you don't need to have a healthy diet, and can eat fast food all the time? Well not exactly, that really depends on your personal stance on the subject of food. I have girlfriends who are on strict diets, exercise a few hours per day with the mentality of going down a dress size, yet for years have not succeeded. Yet I, on the other hand, eat anything and everything I want, rarely exercise, and seem to stay a small size. Others around me have also noticed the happier I get, the slimmer I get without any effort or intention to lose any weight.

So my advice is take your focus off your food, and once again put it on your emotional guidance system. When you pick up an apple, does the thought of biting into it feel good or do you dread it? I personally am not a fan of apples, and for years forced myself to eat them based on how wonderful everyone said they are. I now know better, and unless I genuinely get excited about eating apples, I don't go near them. If I had known back then what I know now, I would have never gone through such an unpleasant diet detox with the naturopath, which ultimately failed to help me. And the exact reason why it failed was my discomfort with the whole idea of cutting out so much of what I love to eat. I didn't want the detox, yet I went ahead with it thinking it was good for me. However, after finishing the detox, I had a new appreciation for vegetables, which I previously used to avoid like the plague.

So before you go and force yourself through another diet, whether to lose weight or heal your body, pay more attention to how you feel. Start caring about the way you feel, and put your focus on what is wanted instead of the unwanted. As you do that, your new-found happiness will itself lead to better food choices. There is very little leverage in controlling what goes into your mouth, you get far more leverage by controlling your focus and focusing your attention on what feels better. And once you do feel better, once you are aligned with your Source, any nutritious food you consume will be of far more benefit to you than ever before.

The human brain affects the vibration of everything it focuses on. If focusing on water with a feeling of love changes the crystals of the water, imagine what your focus does to your food. So appreciate and love everything you are about to eat and drink. When you know you're going to eat that cake, at least don't torture your body, by focusing on the calories you are about to consume or how hard you will have to workout at the gym afterwards. The guilt you feel before and after eating the cake is splitting your energy and causing resistance. This resistance prevents your body from burning the calories, not the cake. Stop the mental battle.

One of my biggest challenges was to stop this splitting of my energy over eating (or any other decision I made on a day by day basis). For example, I had read into the chemicals used to create soft drinks, and how they could substitute as household cleaners. At the same time I wanted to drink soft drinks too, so I was constantly in battle with myself. But as I became aware that my energy played a bigger part in my health problems than what I was consuming, I started relaxing and enjoying my food more. We were born to enjoy food and it's so unfortunate that the media constantly comes out with another bit of research that shows the food we have been consuming for generations, is somehow now unhealthy. Ignore what the media says and just milk every bit of joy you can from your diet, and as you become happier, you will naturally be drawn to foods that are better for you.

My two cents on sugar

The one thing I would advise against is artificial sweeteners, because of their side effects and ability to stop the brain from emitting high vibrations. The rule of thumb here should be, if something is sweet but its packaging says 'no sugar', put it back on the shelf and walk away. There is a pretty good chance it contains artificial sweeteners, and almost all 'diet' soft drinks and 'no sugar' foods these days contain them. These sweeteners are marketed under different names and I don't want to put too much focus on them by listing them here. Just remember real sugar is far better for you than the artificial stuff, so don't kid yourself by thinking your sugar-free drink which is clearly sweet (with harsh chemical sweeteners), is actually healthier for you.

For women on the pill

I don't feel I can finish this book, without sharing what I know about the contraceptive pill, which I was prescribed in my teens as a superficial solution to deeper physiological and emotional imbalances.

> "Today, 10 million women are on the pill, and 82% of us have taken it at some point in our lives. The birth control pill is a $22-billion-a-year industry, with sixty brands now on the market." (Rachel Friedman 2012)

And 1.5 million women in the US take oral contraceptive pills solely for non-contraceptive reasons, such as relief from menstrual pain, treatment of acne, and menstrual irregularity.

But because the pill, or any other medication for that matter, does not treat the underlying cause of the illness, the condition is not really improved, but made to appear improved. The pill accomplishes this through the simulation of normal menstruations each month, so that women think they are having a healthy flow each month, when in fact the menstruation was not due to her own bodily hormones but the synthetic digested hormones. Most doctors, however, do not educate their patient about what is really going on, and she then becomes highly dependent on the pill, as stopping it often leads to even more hormonal imbalances. As I explained in part 1, the pill stops your natural hormones being absorbed by blocking your hormone receptors. It can even cause cancer and infertility in some women, which is rarely if never discussed with women.

While I agree that the intention of many women on the pill is to avoid pregnancy, there are still vast numbers of prescriptions being written, to cover up (whoops, I meant treat!) an array of hormonal imbalances.

"According to the Guttmacher Institute study, the non-contraceptive use of birth-control pills is highest among teenagers. In fact, some 82% of fifteen- to nineteen-year-olds who use OCPs say they do so partly for non-contraceptive reasons, and 33% of these teens report using them strictly for these reasons." (Rachel Friedman 2012)

And these are just the physiological effects of the pill. What about the psychological effects? Anxiety, depression and, in my case, extreme anger. What about changing women's pheromones so much that they are attracted to men with whom they are not genetically compatible, and then go on to conceive?

If you are thinking to yourself that some women don't experience these side effects, yes I agree. At the end of the day, your emotional state is what determines your body's ability to heal and repair itself or not. I am the first to admit my hormonal imbalances for which I was prescribed the pill had their roots in my emotional state. But I still feel it is my duty to point out to females that **the pill is not a cure, it is a Band-Aid for something unbalanced much deeper.**

And for the gentlemen reading this book? Please support the women in your lives by encouraging them to look for natural ways of healing. You will find your partners without the pill to be far happier and healthier.

I managed to finally stop the pill after well over a decade at age twenty-five. And with the help of a wonderful acupuncturist and Chinese medicine, my hormones are now balanced, and I no longer have symptoms of PCOS. There is such empowerment in taking your health into your own hands, and I wish for you to feel as happy as I feel.

"You are a volume in the divine book
A mirror to the power that created the
    Universe
Whatever you want, ask it of yourself
Whatever you're looking for can only
    be found inside of you"

—Rumi

CHAPTER 7

Where to from here?

I started out in my twenties, living pretty unconsciously even though I had seen my thoughts and words effect my life. So I clearly needed major wake-up calls to get me on the right track again. The wake-up calls came in many forms, but the most painful were in my body.

I have now reached a point in my life where I don't resent what I went through any longer. I have no regrets, not only because it doesn't feel good to have regrets but also because of the awareness I now have. The understanding I've gained as a consequence of what I went through has changed every area of my life. My relationships, my career, my finances have all had massive improvements because of my newly-found and sustained elevated emotional state. Actually the more I think about it the more I start to appreciate my journey, because what I now know has had a enormously positive impact on my family and friends who have also started changing their thoughts and watching the 'miracles' show up. Life is a game, a game that has rules that we have not been taught fully. If you learn these rules, you are able to enjoy the game and thrive. If you don't know the rules, it's going to be a difficult ride, and you begin to think outside forces such as luck and destiny are defining your success.

I will never forget what these health challenges have taught me about the power of our mind in creating our reality. The journey I went through as a consequence of the illnesses has taught me much more than how to heal myself. I have taken my power back and learnt what a potent creator I am. I have finally reached a point where I am able to truly appreciate all my pain and suffering, because they led me to the wonderful place I am now, a place where I love what I see in the mirror, I enjoy the health and vitality of my body, I revel in its ability to find its own balance, without the need for external help. It is wonderful to exercise without any pain. It is fabulous to move without any discomfort. It's reassuring to sit among a group of people with the seasonal flu and know only my emotional state determines if I'm at risk or not. And every time I drive past my local medical centre knowing I'm no longer a regular, I am speechless in appreciation. There is so much pleasure in knowing that you will never again be a helpless victim. It is hard-earned wisdom, but most certainly worth it, because I can now help others get to their destination of wellbeing more quickly. I took the path least travelled, and discovered a whole new way of joyous living.

Just as this book is coming to a completion, I've received my yearly eye test results, and its absolutely thrilling. In the past three years, my eyesight has improved extremely. Since school I was short-sighted (myopic) and had to wear prescription glasses. Then in 2009, as I started focusing on my health and was no longer on any medications I thought wouldn't it be nice if I didn't need to wear glasses any more and my eyes healed naturally? I wasn't sure how it could be done, and I certainly wasn't going to ask my optometrist, who only believed your eyes worsen with age. Yet I kept that intention alive within me. Both eyes were 1.5 at the time. In 2010 during my yearly test (by another optometrist), I was ecstatic to see my eyes had become 1.0 and 1.25. The improvement was not massive, but certainly worth celebrating. I was initially naïve enough to show my 2010 results to the original optometrist, who concluded there was no way my eyes could have improved, and that surely the new optometrist had made a mistake. At that point I came to the clear conclusion that I should avoid discussing my medical results with anyone in the future, until I am solid enough in my beliefs not to get upset by their opinions. I continued to expect more improvements in 2011, which is exactly what happened. My new eye reading was 1.0 on both eyes, I was very happy. As my body started showing more signs of healing, my belief in my eyes healing naturally raised. And my 2012 eye test results read 0.5 and 0.75. Not only is this great progress, but this one incident has certainly caught the attention of my family and friends. While I would like to scream **"I did it myself, I reversed my eyesight!"** all I really did was keep the intention alive within me. I was willing to give my body a stress-free environment, and my body took care of the rest.

I'm sure my journey of spiritual awakening has only just begun, and like many it has begun as a consequence of not being satisfied with the status quo. Maybe if I had been content enough with just consuming medicine for the rest of my life, I would have never come to such a clear understanding of the role I play in my reality. I would have never known how good it feels to be a deliberate creator of my own reality, as Abraham has taught. I would have never grasped how the Source Energy that is present within me is also the same Source Energy that has created the Universe. It is for this reason that I know I have embarked on an exhilarating and fascinating adventure towards fully understanding the relationship between my physical self and my much greater metaphysical self.

I look forward to more learning on my way towards more happiness and joy. And I hope that you too begin to enjoy your own unique path towards wellbeing. I feel so much appreciation for the time you have taken to spend with me on my journey.

You are awesome and loved more than you will ever know.

"And you? When will you begin that
long journey into yourself?"

—Rumi

Cheat Sheet

- Go where you are being pulled. If you feel an urge to call someone, do it. If it feels good to read a book, read it. Follow even the smallest good feeling thoughts and inspirations. By practising listening to your feelings, you are effectively exercising your sensitivity to your feelings. The more you do this, the better you will get at recognising even slight feelings, which is how your guidance system communicates with you.

- Milk every positive thing in your life. Make it your daily intention to look for the good in your life, the people around you, your home, your body, your car. Find things to feel good about and soon the Universe will give you more and more good feeling reasons.

- Expect things to go well for you. Start small, like expecting the drive to work to be pleasant. Or expect the department store queue to be short. Then work your way up to bigger expectations. Your expectations prepare your reality for you in unbelievable ways. Make your way to work every morning imagining how your day might turn out. How do you want interactions to go with colleagues? How much fun will your day be? How productive will you be?

- Your thought vibrations are magnetic. The more emotion is attached to a thought, the more its magnetic power. Happy joyous thoughts bring more happy joyous things into your life.

So pay close attention to how you feel at any moment, and watch as the world around you responds to your emotional state.

- You attract by your attention (powered by emotion) to a subject. It doesn't matter if you say you don't want X or you do want X. It is your underlying emotion that determines the outcome, not the words you use.

- Unknowingly you have attracted your current physical condition. Knowing you did it means you can also undo it. You and you alone hold the key to your healing. Keep raising your emotions, and look for reasons to feel better. As you do, your cells will begin to also repair themselves.

- Your DNA resonates most with love, so try to find more reasons to love, and 'miracles' will take place in your body. Remember that a miracle is just something that science doesn't yet have an explanation for. And there is a lot out there that science is yet to discover.

- When you have a positive thought of someone, make no mistake that they are receiving your vibrations. So when you make a nasty comment about your boss (and you keep up that feeling long enough), guess what your boss will feel towards you? She or he may not know it, but the vibrations of your thoughts towards them are certainly received.

- Start every day with the intention to find more and more things to feel good about, and watch as your life keeps getting better and better.

- Use the buffer of time to your advantage. Keep focusing on what you want, and refining your idea of the manifestations you have been asking for. If you don't keep molding or refining this vision, when it manifests it will often not be exactly as you now want.

- Assume the best about people and circumstances, and you will always get the best out of them.

- If there is still a bit of your illness left, it's because there is still something you are pushing against. In some area of your life you are still trying to make things happen with action, while your energy is not yet lined up, causing resistance. Focus instead on what brings you joy.

- Follow your good feelings and impulses. Your good feelings are your Source's way of directing you towards everything you want. Listen to these impulses, you will be rewarded in amazing ways.

- Watch more comedy and feel good movies. Avoid anything that does not bring you joy, whether it's people or media. Treat yourself with care during this healing phase.

- All matter is made up of the same atoms, but with different vibrations. The only thing that distinguishes one flower's colour from another is its vibrational frequency. This is why, when your vibrational frequency changes, so does your appearance, health, relationship and abundance.

- Remember that your brain affects the vibration of everything you focus on. So appreciate and love everything you are about to eat and drink. You know you're going to eat that ice cream, so why torture your body by putting yourself through a guilt trip? Don't count the calories you are about to consume or how hard you will have to workout at the gym afterwards. The guilt you feel before and after eating the ice cream is splitting your energy and causing resistance, and it's that resistance that causes you problems, not the ice cream. Stop the mental battle.

- Protect your dream of wellbeing. Others around you may not understand how you can accomplish self-healing and will trample over your dream before it becomes a reality. Instead lead by example, heal yourself and let your success light the way for others.